D0532952

18 Ways to Play Better Golf

Mental Preparation for Peak Performance

Antoine Nguyen, M. A.

www.total-performance.ca
"Performance enhancement through mental preparation, discipline, and toughness"
Information, tips, and articles on peak performance in sports

ISBN 0-7414-1410-4

Published by:
INFINITY
PUBLISHING.COM
519 West Lancaster Avenue
Haverford, PA 19041-1413
Info@buybooksontheweb.com
www.buybooksontheweb.com
Toll-free (877) BUY BOOK
Local Phone (610) 520-2500
Fax (610) 519-0261

Printed in the United States of America

Printed on Recycled Paper

Published March 2003

Contents

Introduction . . . . -I-

Hole #1
    Self-Awareness . . . . -1-

Hole #2
    Goal-Setting . . . . -15-

Hole #3
    Process vs Outcome Thinking . . . . -23-

Hole #4
    Self-Beliefs . . . . -31-

Hole #5
    Self-Talk . . . . -37-

Hole #6
    Mental Imagery . . . . -47-

Hole #7
    Confidence . . . . -59-

Hole #8
    Composure . . . . -71-

Hole #9
    Concentration . . . . -85-

The Cantina . . . . -103-

Hole #10
    Basic Principles . . . . -105-

Hole #11
    Anchoring . . . . -113-

Hole #12
    Performance Routines .... -121-

Hole #13
    Self-Monitoring .... -131-

Hole #14
    Practice .... -141-

Hole #15
    Preparation .... -151-

Hole #16
    Mental Plans .... -165-

Hole #17
    Putting .... -175-

Hole #18
    Specific Problems .... -185-

Scorecard .... -195-

The 19ᵗʰ Hole .... -197-

Appendix A
    Performance Profile Chart .... -201-
    Competition Evaluation .... -203-
    Goal-Setting Form .... -207-
    Self-Belief Chart .... -209-
    Self-Talk Log .... -211-
    Self-Talk Change Chart .... -213-
    Positive Affirmation List .... -215-
    Personal Achievement List .... -217-
    Distraction Control Chart .... -219-
    Refocusing Chart .... -221-
    Post-Round Evaluation .... -223-
    Preparation Chart .... -227-
    Pre-Competition Plan .... -229-

Critical Situation Chart . . . . -231-

Appendix B
Relaxation Script . . . . -233-

Introduction

Over the last few years, there has been an increasing recognition from top Amateur and Professional athletes about the importance of mental skills in peak performance. Top athletes in all sports have strong concentration skills, high composure, and unshakable confidence. It is this mental toughness that sets them apart from other equally skilled athletes.

Most golfers will admit that golf is 80 or 90% mental, yet most spend all their time and efforts on the mechanical aspect of their game. Today, we know more about the golf swing than we ever did, yet the average handicap for club players is still the same now as it was 20 years ago, even with all the new technology in equipment and video analysis.

Many golfers think that it takes a perfect swing to play well and thus spend all their time striving for technical perfection, but seldom do they think about how the mind affects performance. You must realize that almost no one has a perfect swing, not even the pros. Striving for technical perfection is a lot harder than learning to think well. Each of us has a certain way of swinging the club that matches our physical attributes and personality. Of course, there are some fundamental rules that apply to every good swing, but the goal is to hit the ball as straight and far as you can, not how gracefully you do it.

During a round, with so little time spent on actually executing a shot, the mental aspect of golf is crucial to success. If the mind was not that important, then why do so many golfers hit good shots when practicing, but not on the course? Why do they play great golf one day, but poorly the next? Why do they play well on the front nine but poorly on the back nine? And all the while there are no changes in physical ability. The fact is: your mind and body are connected and work together, so how you think will affect how you perform. Evidently, the mind is a critical determinant in shot making.

Just like physical skills, mental skills can be learned and developed. Confidence, concentration, and composure are at the core of getting the most out of your talent. A good state of mind in itself won't guarantee a low score, but only gives you the best chance of doing so. In other words, the goal is to shoot the best possible score with the swing that you have.

Mental training is not a luxury. It is as necessary as technical and physical skills if you want to become the best golfer you can be. Top athletes have developed these crucial mental skills on their own, but now everyone can do the same through mental training. This book will teach you all the necessary mental skills to take your game to the next level. Not only will strong mental skills help you in golf, but in all other areas of life as well. In a way, these are not just mental skills. These are life skills.

This book is organized into 18 holes (the words "chapters" and "holes" will be used interchangeably throughout the book). Each chapter covers a particular skill and contains exercises and detailed instructions on how to get the most out of your game. The first nine holes cover more general mental skills while the last nine holes cover more integrated and practical strategies incorporating all the skills taught in the front nine.

There are three ways you can read this book. The first and most recommended one is to read the book chapter by chapter, going through all 18 holes. At the beginning of each chapter, you will find a series of questions that will assess your level of competence in the topic discussed. These questions will yield a certain golf score. At the end of the 18 holes, you will have a golf score that reflects your mental skills. The number of strokes you add for each answer (never, sometimes, or always) is indicated on top of the questions. You then take your result and add it to the minimum score for each type of hole. On par 3's, you start with one stroke; on par 4's and 5's, you start with 2 strokes. After a certain amount of training, you can go back to each chapter and answer the questions again to get a new score. Thus, any improvement in your mental game will be reflected in your golf score (in this book AND on the golf course).

The second method is to go directly to the chapters dealing

with your particular needs. If you are not sure what these needs are, go to Hole #1 and complete Exercise 1.4. This exercise will direct you to the appropriate chapters that deal with your particular needs in terms of mental training.

Finally, the third way to use this handbook is to go directly to the back nine and start from there. The last nine chapters is an integration of all the basic skills taught in previous chapters. Each chapter contains references to previous ones so that you can go back and get more information on any specific topic.

Regardless of how you want to use this handbook, you will benefit most from it if you do the included exercises and fill out the forms provided in each chapter as you encounter them. Included in the appendix are all the forms necessary for you to build a mental training log. You might want to make copies of these forms before writing into them, as they might prove useful in the future.

If you are looking for an edge, this book will help you find one. Have a pen ready, and prepare to embark on a journey of self-discovery and excellence.

Hole #1
Self-Awareness

Par 3

Questions
Never: +2 Sometimes: +1 Always: 0

1- I know what my strengths and weaknesses are.
2- I know when I tend to make a bad or good shot.
3- I know what the major difference is between a good and a bad round.

Add 1 stroke to your score
Score:

Self-Awareness

The first step towards any improvement is to understand yourself as a person and as a golfer. Why do I play well? Why do I play poorly? When do I get angry? What makes me lose my focus? What am I afraid of? Before you can change, you need to know who you are and who you want to change into. Hence, you need to have a clear focus of what you need to do and how you need to think to play your best every time you step on the golf course. Not only is this process necessary for mental training, but for technical skills as well. What are your strengths and weaknesses? Once you've identified those, you can start building on your strengths and improve your weaknesses. That is when improvement will occur.

Exercise 1.1: Performance Profile

First start by thinking of the ideal golfer. What are the physical, technical, and mental abilities of the ideal golfer. What skills does one need to become the ultimate golfer? These ideal skills can be the following: great short game, accurate shots, staying calm under pressure, high confidence, high concentration, reliable putter, good temper, or good tactical judgement. Then, give a rating from 1 to 10 for each of these qualities, 10 being a very important quality, and 1 being not important at all. Usually, almost everything would get a rating of 10.

Second, rate your current level on a scale of 1 to 10 for each of those qualities. Be as honest as you can because these ratings will determine what needs immediate improvement. Once you've done this, examine the difference between the ideal golfer and your current status. Subtract your current rating from your ideal rating. The higher the difference, the higher the priority for improvement.

Table 1.1
Sample Performance Profile

Quality	Ideal Rating	Current Rating	Difference
Short game	10	6	4
Confidence	10	6	4
Concentration	10	7	3
Composure	9	4	5
Shot Accuracy	10	5	5
Putting	10	8	2
Tactical Judgement	9	6	3

According to this profile, our imaginary golfer would need to set shot accuracy and composure as high priority areas. Next in line would be the short game and confidence. Thus, by doing this sort of profiling, you'll get a good idea of your strengths and weaknesses. Go ahead and fill out a table similar to Table 1.1 now (a blank table can be found in Appendix A, p.201).

Now that you have a better idea of your strengths and weaknesses, you also need to find out why you play well and why you play poorly. This can be done by examining your best and worst performances.

Exercise 1.2: Best & Worst Performance

A.   Think about your best performance ever in golf. It can be an entire round, half a round, or a single hole. Relive that performance now. Try to recreate every sight, sound, and feeling associated with that performance. What were the main

Self-Awareness

reasons for this great performance? What did you do prior to the round / hole? What were you thinking about? Where was your focus? What were you doing or saying to yourself? To assist you with this exercise, here are some questions you can answer.

1. Circle your feeling *going into this round.*

No anxiety   0 1 2 3 4 5 6 7 8 9 10   Very anxious

No physical   0 1 2 3 4 5 6 7 8 9 10   Highly activated
activation (flat)   and pumped up

2. Rate your level of Confidence in this round:

No confidence   0 1 2 3 4 5 6 7 8 9 10   Completely confident

What was the main reason(s) responsible for this confidence level?

3. Rate your level of Concentration in this round:

No concentration   0 1 2 3 4 5 6 7 8 9 10   Completely concentrated

What was the main reason(s) responsible for this concentration level?

4. Rate your level of Composure in this round:

No composure   0 1 2 3 4 5 6 7 8 9 10   Very composed

What was the main reason(s) responsible for this composure level?

Self-Awareness

5. What were you saying to yourself or thinking shortly before the start of that round?

6. What were you paying attention to or focusing on during that round?

B. Now, think about your worst performance. Relive every aspect of that performance now. What were the main reasons responsible for this poor performance? What did you do prior to the round / hole? What were you thinking about? Where was your focus? What were you doing or saying to yourself? Write this information down in the space below.

7. Circle your feeling *going into this round/hole.*

No anxiety   0 1 2 3 4 5 6 7 8 9 10   Very anxious

No physical   0 1 2 3 4 5 6 7 8 9 10   Highly activated
activation (flat)   and pumped up

8. Rate your level of Confidence in this round/hole:

No confidence   0 1 2 3 4 5 6 7 8 9 10   Completely confident

What was the main reason(s) responsible for this confidence level?

9. Rate your level of Concentration in this round/hole:

No concentration   0 1 2 3 4 5 6 7 8 9 10   Completely concentrated

What was the main reason(s) responsible for this concentration level?

10. Rate your level of Composure in this round/hole:

Self-Awareness

No composure   0   1   2   3   4   5   6   7   8   9   10   Very composed

What was the main reason(s) responsible for this composure level?

11. What were you saying to yourself or thinking shortly before the start of that round/hole?

12. What were you paying attention to of focusing on during that round/hole?

C. What seems to be the major difference between your best and worst performance?

13. In what you were thinking prior to that round/hole?

14. In what you were focused on during that round/hole?

15. How would you prefer to feel before each round/hole?

No anxiety   0   1   2   3   4   5   6   7   8   9   10   Very anxious

No physical   0   1   2   3   4   5   6   7   8   9   10   Highly activated
activation (flat)   and pumped up

16. How would you prefer to focus your attention during each round/hole?

17. How would you prefer to approach each round/hole?

Hopefully, this exercise has provided you with important insights about the causes and circumstances surrounding your best and worst performances (form also found in Appendix A, p.203). The goal, of course, is to recreate the optimal mindset and make every round a good round.

While this gives you information on how you need to think during a hole or an entire round, you also need to know what allows you to make a good shot. Since golf must be played one shot at a time, you need to think about every shot, not just an entire round or a hole. The following exercise will help you uncover the clues that will direct your attention on what is important in making a shot.

Exercise 1.3

Find a quiet place and get yourself into a comfortable position. Now, think of a successful shot you've made in the past. It can be a perfect drive down the middle of the fairway, an approach shot that hit the pin, or a perfect putt for a birdie. Try to recreate that shot as vividly as possible in your mind. First see it as if you were watching a highlight reel. Notice every detail surrounding you as you were setting up for the shot. See the hole, the distance to the pin, the light and shadows, the trees, the grass. Now, jump into your body and see it through your own eyes. Look at every detail again from your own eyes, as if you were actually there. What were you thinking about? What were you focused on? Now hit the shot. Hear the sound of the club striking the ball, feel the sensation of the sweet contact of a perfect swing. Pay attention to the loudness of the sounds. Feel your body move as you went through the different steps of the swing. What did you see, what were you thinking about?

Replay the shot and, again, notice the cues you were focused on. Was it the back of the ball, your target, or a particular swing thought? How were you feeling? Were you nervous or calm? Notice the tension and energy in your muscles. Pay attention to how each part of your body felt as you were going through the swing.

Replay the shot again and again, each time trying to glean more information on how you felt, what you were thinking, where you were focusing. You can even fast forward or rewind this mental "video tape" as you please. See what it feels like to hit 5 shots in a second. Write every detail that you judge important for the success of this shot in the space below now.

Now that you have information on your strengths and weaknesses as well as how you should prepare, think, and focus before each round, hole, and shot, you are ready to improve your game.

If you intend to go through every "hole" in this handbook, then skip the following exercise. The same questions found in this exercise can be found before each chapter. However, if you want to have a quick assessment of mental areas where you need improvement and read the chapter concerned with it only, then this exercise will direct you to the appropriate chapter(s) so that you can improve your game right away.

Exercise 1.4: Golf Information Form

Goal-Setting

1. I set clear daily and yearly goals.   Never _____ Always
                                        1 2 3 4 5 6 7

2. I have specific goals that are measurable.   Never _____ Always
                                          1 2 3 4 5 6 7

3. I set short-term performance goals leading   Never _____ Always
to long-term goals.   1 2 3 4 5 6 7

If you have a score **below 15**, go to Hole # 2 .

Preparation

1. I come to the course early to stretch and   Never _____ Always
warm-up before a round.   1 2 3 4 5 6 7

2. I play well right from the beginning of a round. Never _____ Always

1 2 3 4 5 6 7

3. I follow a consistent warm-up plan before a round. Never _____ Always

1 2 3 4 5 6 7

If your score is **below 15**, consider going to Hole # 15.

Practice

1. I have a clear plan when I practice. Never _____ Always

1 2 3 4 5 6 7

2. I have a clear goal for each practice Never _____ Always

1 2 3 4 5 6 7

3. I hit as well on the course than at practice. Never _____ Always

1 2 3 4 5 6 7

4. Each time I practice, I spend at least 60% of my time working on my short game. Never _____ Always

1 2 3 4 5 6 7

5. I pick a target and go through my preshot routine at practice. Never _____ Always

1 2 3 4 5 6 7

If you scored **below 25**, go to Hole # 14.

Confidence

1. I lose confidence if I didn't hit well during the warm-up. Never _____ Always

1 2 3 4 5 6 7

2. I think about swing mechanics before hitting because I can't trust my swing. Never _____ Always

1 2 3 4 5 6 7

3. I lose confidence after a bad start. Never _____ Always

1 2 3 4 5 6 7

4. I don't feel confident before hitting. Never _____ Always

1 2 3 4 5 6 7

If you scored **above 20**, go to Hole # 7.

Composure

1. I have trouble sinking pressure putts. Never _____ Always

1 2 3 4 5 6 7

2. I am anxious when there is water or sand nearby. Never _____ Always

1 2 3 4 5 6 7

Self-Awareness

3. I get frustrated when play slows down.   Never ＿＿＿＿＿＿＿＿＿ Always
                                              1 2 3 4 5 6 7

4. I get angry after a bad shot.   Never ＿＿＿＿＿＿＿＿＿ Always
                                              1 2 3 4 5 6 7

5. Once I get angry or frustrated, I find it Never ＿＿＿＿＿＿＿＿＿ Always
hard to regain control of my game.   1 2 3 4 5 6 7

If you scored **above 25**, go to Hole # 8.

Concentration

1. I get distracted when there are people   Never ＿＿＿＿＿＿＿＿＿ Always
watching.   1 2 3 4 5 6 7

2. I let my daily hassles affect my game on the   Never ＿＿＿＿＿＿＿＿＿ Always
course.   1 2 3 4 5 6 7

3. I think about past mistakes or have   Never ＿＿＿＿＿＿＿＿＿ Always
difficulty forgetting them.   1 2 3 4 5 6 7

4. I think about the consequences of   Never ＿＿＿＿＿＿＿＿＿ Always
making or missing a shot.   1 2 3 4 5 6 7

5. I am distracted when the group behind   Never ＿＿＿＿＿＿＿＿＿ Always
is catching up.   1 2 3 4 5 6 7

If you scored **above 25**, go to Hole # 9.

Imagery

1. I can visualize the line on my putts.   Never ＿＿＿＿＿＿＿＿＿ Always
                                              1 2 3 4 5 6 7

2. I mentally replay my best shots before hitting.   Never ＿＿＿＿＿＿＿＿＿ Always
                                              1 2 3 4 5 6 7

3. I can easily see or feel myself   Never ＿＿＿＿＿＿＿＿＿ Always
executing a perfect shot.   1 2 3 4 5 6 7

4. I have positive images/thoughts in my mind   Never ＿＿＿＿＿＿＿＿＿ Always
before or during my swing.   1 2 3 4 5 6 7

If you scored **below 20**, go to Hole # 6.

Self-Awareness

Self-Talk

1. I have cue words to direct my attention
and refocus.

Never _____ Always

    1 2 3 4 5 6 7

2. I encourage myself with positive statements.

Never _____ Always

    1 2 3 4 5 6 7

3. I say positive things to myself after a bad shot.

Never _____ Always

    1 2 3 4 5 6 7

If your score is **below 15**, consider going to Hole # 5.

Process Thinking

1. I think about winning when I play.

Never _____ Always

    1 2 3 4 5 6 7

2. I keep track of my score and what I can shoot
after each hole.

Never _____ Always

    1 2 3 4 5 6 7

3. I am not satisfied unless I shoot a certain score.

Never _____ Always

    1 2 3 4 5 6 7

If your score is **above 15**, consider going to hole # 3.

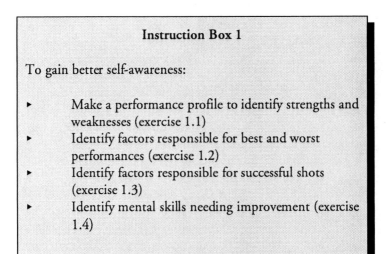

Instruction Box 1

To gain better self-awareness:

- Make a performance profile to identify strengths and weaknesses (exercise 1.1)
- Identify factors responsible for best and worst performances (exercise 1.2)
- Identify factors responsible for successful shots (exercise 1.3)
- Identify mental skills needing improvement (exercise 1.4)

Hole #2
Goal-Setting

Par 4

Questions
Never: +2 Sometimes: +1 Always: 0

1- I set clear daily goals.
2- I have specific goals that are measurable.
3- I set short-term performance goals leading to long-term goals.
4- I set goals for practice and for golf rounds.

Add 2 strokes to your score
Score:

Goal-Setting

Goals are aims or objectives that we consciously set out to achieve or accomplish. They give our efforts direction and provide us with a mean of organizing our immediate and distant future. We all set goals, but most of the time they're not formulated in a way that push us to achieve. While winning or "becoming a better golfer" are worthwhile goals, they do not specify how or what one should do in order to perform better.

The basic theoretical assumption is that specific and difficult goals lead to higher levels of performance than "do your best" goals. Consequently, many people set goals that are too general and easy ("do my best", "I want to be better at this", "I just want to have fun out there") and thus, don't really benefit from goal-setting. These goals are also not measurable, and the way to achieve them is not defined. For example, you'll often hear a golfer who is in a slump say: "I'll just have to work harder". Just what does working harder give you? One needs to define what aspect of the game one has to work on, and then spend more time working on it at practice. On the other hand, performance goals such as "drive the fairway 70% of the time" and "hit the green 90% of the time when within a 100 yards or less" are specific and measurable, thus can direct your attention to improving these aspects of your game. By setting these kinds of goals, you can identify weak aspects in your game and focus your efforts in improving them.

Another common mistake is to be too focused on outcome goals (i.e., "I want to win this competition"). Outcome goals such as winning or shooting a certain score are useful in that they can energize and motivate us, but the means to get to the end are not defined. Performance goals such as "spend 70% of practice time on short game" or "drive the fairway 80% of the time", as well as specific objective goals such as "hit 14 greens in regulation" are more effective goals because they direct our efforts to specific areas of performance that are measurable. In addition, setting short-term goals to achieve long-term goals is much more beneficial than long-term goals alone. An analogy can be drawn to a staircase, where climbing up small steps is easier than trying to jump all the way to the top. Finally, commitment to achieve your goals is essential. Without commitment, goals are useless. They become nothing more than dreams or fantasies.

In sum, goals help direct attention, mobilize effort, increase long-term persistence and promote development of new strategies. To be effective, goals should be difficult, specific, and measurable. Goal-setting can be an art that is difficult to master at first, but when done properly, can be one of the most effective tools to increase motivation and enhance performance.

Summary Box 2.1

Benefits of Goal-Setting:
- ► Improved performance
- ► Improved confidence & satisfaction
- ► Higher motivation
- ► Clear expectations & focus
- ► Greater sense of purpose
- ► Decreased anxiety
- ► Greater practice quality
- ► Better time-management

<u>Guidelines for Goal-Setting</u>

- *Set Specific and Measurable Goals*: Specific numerical goals are more effective than "do your best" or "becoming better" goals. Example of such goals are: hitting 12 greens in regulation, hit 90% of chip shots within 3 feet or less of the cup, or spending 1 hour each day hitting wedge shots.

- *Set Difficult but Realistic Goals*: There is a direct relationship between goal difficulty and performance as long as the difficulty of the goal does not exceed your abilities. Difficult goals challenge us to stretch our limits and develop new strategies and skills to achieve greater performance. When goals are too easy, we tend to stay in our comfort zone and do only the minimum necessary to achieve these goals.

- *Set both Long-Term and Short-Term Goals*: Small steps lead to higher levels. While long-term goals provide us with a greater vision, short-term goals provide us with the means of achieving those long-term objectives. Short-term goals help us keep long-term goals in sight and provide immediate feedback on our progression. Increased motivation is also provided by short-term goals because we can see immediate and steady improvement. Remember, little goals lead to big dreams.

- *Set Performance Goals rather than Outcome Goals*: Outcome goals have been shown to be less effective than performance goals because they don't provide us with any direction as to what should be done to achieve them. We cannot fully control outcomes, thus we set ourselves up for possible failure which could affect confidence and motivation. Performance goals, on the other hand, are under our control and can be achieved regardless of outcome. Success or failure can be assessed on the sole basis of performance, which is the only thing under our control.

- *Set Practice Goals as well as Game Goals*: Practice goals are important because this is where improvement will occur. The amount of time spent in practice should be purposeful and of the highest quality. Thus, having goals for practice is essential to keep motivation high and direct your efforts to weaker areas. Game goals are important because they are the basis by which you will measure improvement.

- *Set Positive Goals rather than Negative Goals*: Whenever possible, try to state goals in positive terms instead of negative terms. You should define what you want to happen instead of what you don't want to happen (i.e., "hit 80% of fairways" instead of "don't miss more than 20% of fairways"). Positive goal-setting will make you focus on success instead of failure.

- *Set Target Dates for Attaining Goals*: Target dates motivate you to expand more effort to achieve your goals and prevents procrastination.

An easy way to remember some of these important guidelines is to use the S.M.A.R.T. acronym (Specific, Measurable, Adjustable, Realistic, Time-based).

Summary Box 2.2

Guidelines for setting goals:

▸   Set specific and measurable goals
▸   Set difficult but realistic goals
▸   Set both long-term and short-term goals
▸   Set performance goals instead of outcome goals
▸   Set practice and game goals
▸   Set positive goals instead of negative goals
▸   Set target dates for attaining goals

Goals can be either physical, technical, or mental. Once you have set your goals, you need to outline a strategy to achieve these goals and give yourself a deadline for each. Finally, remember that you can set new goals every day (or every week) or modify existing ones along the way. Be committed to achieving these goals and reward yourself for successes.

It's best to write down your goals in order to have a physical reminder to direct your attention day after day. A sample of a goal-setting form can be found on the next page.

Goal-Setting

Table 2.1
Sample Goal-Setting Form

Skill area to be improved	Specific Goal(s)	Strategy	Evaluation Date	Conclusion
Chips	Hit 80% of chips within 3 feet of the cup	- practice chipping for 30 minutes each day - improve feel by doing kinesthetic imagery every day - develop a chipping routine - try to hole it every time - use self-talk	- June 11 - After each Round	Partial success -- achieved goal for June 11, but still too many erratic rounds.
Concentration	Get a score of 48 or more for concentration on psychological scorecard	- Develop preshot routine - Use post-shot routine - Park bad shots	-After each round - June 5	complete success
Putts	Make 28 putts or less	- practice putting for 20 minutes each day - develop pre-putt routine	After each round	success
Practice	Spend 75% of time in performance mentality	- execute preshot routine before each shot - simulate round conditions	May 28	success

Exercise 2.1: Goal-Setting

Think about what you want to achieve this year and fill out the blank goal-setting form at the end of this handbook (Appendix A, p.207).

Instruction Box 2

- ▸ Think about what you want to achieve
- ▸ Set long-term goals
- ▸ Set short-term goals leading to long-term goals
- ▸ Elaborate strategies to achieve those goals
- ▸ Evaluate your goals

Hole #3
Process vs Outcome Thinking

Par 3

Questions
Never: 0 Sometimes: +1 Always: +2

1- I think about winning or score when I play.
2- I keep track of my score and what I can shoot after each hole.
3- I need to shoot a certain score to enjoy myself

Add 1 stroke to your score
Score:

Process vs Outcome Thinking

The reason most of us started playing golf was because of the challenge and fun it provided. We enjoyed the pleasure of being outdoors in the company of friends, to get away from urban life and the stress of work, and to experience the occasional exhilaration of hitting a perfect shot. Who couldn't remember his/her first solid drive? When you hit that first perfect shot, that's when you become addicted to golf. From there on, we embark on a quest for that elusive joy and sense of mastery that great golf creates. But somewhere along the road, the pure joy of golf gives way to pressure and frustration that are the result of perfectionism, expectations, fear of failure, and anxiety. Soon, a Sunday afternoon golf round becomes an event filled with anger, frustration, stress, and despair. We come to resent the very challenges which made us love golf in the first place. Most of the time, this happens when we start playing golf for results or achievements (outcome) instead of playing for the sheer fun and challenge of each shot (process).

The challenges that golf presents us with are unique. At a competitive level, golf may be the only sport where we will always loose more than we win. Therefore, it becomes important to attribute less importance to outcomes if we want to keep our motivation and confidence.

"When will I break 90?", "When will I be a scratch golfer?", "When will I win my first tournament?", are questions that often create additional pressure and take away the fun that each round of golf can provide us with. Some people don't have any fun unless they break 80. If they don't, they just see it as another wasted round. Watching certain people on the golf course, you'd swear that they were forced at gunpoint to play golf rather then playing because they wanted to enjoy themselves and have a pleasant time. If you can't have fun, then why keep playing?

It's easy to fall into the trap of playing for results instead of playing for the intrinsic pleasure of playing itself, especially for good golfers or competitive golfers. Everything surrounding us encourages outcome thinking. But if people could enjoy themselves more on the golf course, they would have much better results. I'm not saying that outcomes are not important. For the golfer who's livelihood depends on how well he performs, results are what determines if he'll make money or keep his PGA card. Although outcomes are important (since golf is a game on which outcome alone dictates whether or not you make $200,000 or $100), a focus based on process is what will bring about the best outcome. Golfers who emphasize outcome will experience a lot of ups and downs in their game, while golfers who emphasize the process have greater consistency and can enjoy themselves even when they don't win. A positive outlook that stems from process-thinking allows you to avoid long slumps.

You cannot control outcomes, so why waste energy trying to control what cannot be controlled? The only thing you can control is how you hit each shot. If you go into a tournament expecting to win, then you're setting yourself up for deception. You may *believe* you can win, but your focus should not be on winning but on doing what it takes to win. For example, you may have played a great round of golf, but don't feel bad because someone else played a better round. Similarly, you were hitting the ball well, but you just didn't have the right breaks and played over 80. Enjoy the fact that you were hitting the ball great instead of berating yourself for yet another failure. You can't let poor results undermine your confidence and your fun. Many great golfers such as Bobby Jones, Jack Nicklaus, Nick Price, and Bernhard Langer did not achieve consistent success until they freed themselves of winning expectations and outcome thinking. Again, an important distinction has to be made between *believing* that one could win and *focusing* on winning. These golfers believed that they could win, but they did not think about winning once they were playing.

So what exactly is process thinking? Process thinking involves enjoying the inherent challenges of the game and staying focused in the face of adversity, playing one shot at a time and concentrating on what needs to be done in the here-and-now, and judging success for how well you played in every facet of the game rather than on the final results.

It's important to note that it's not an either-or situation. You are not outcome OR process-oriented. Your mode of thinking can be viewed on a continuum, where outcome and process are at each end of this continuum. You have a dominant mode of thinking which tends to lean more towards one end or the other on this continuum. Sometimes, given certain circumstances, you will move more towards outcome thinking, while at other times, you may be more process-oriented.

Exercise 3.1

Answer the following questions:

1. What is my dominant mode of thinking?

2. When do I tend to become outcome-oriented?

3. What are the reasons or circumstances promoting outcome-thinking?

4. What happens when I focus too much on outcome or results?

Suggestions for achieving process thinking

▸ *Maintain your focus in the present:* Focus on each shot and don't dwell on previous shots or think about upcoming ones. Don't think about the consequences of making or missing a shot. Just concentrate on playing one shot at a time and don't think about the score you'll shoot.

▸ *Develop a good preshot routine:* A good preshot routine will allow you to be focused on each shot, regardless of external circumstances. This prevents your mind from drifting to unwanted thoughts about score and winning that will distract you from the task at hand, which is the shot that you immediately have to make (for more on preshot routines, see Chapter 12)

▸ *Let your partner write your score:* If you're not writing your score, you won't think about it as much. Let someone else hold the scorecard, and don't try to keep track of what you're shooting. Tell that person to keep you ignorant of your score until the end of the round.

▸ *Don't count your score after the front nine:* Again, this will ensure that you'll play the back nine with a free and quiet mind. Knowing what you shot on the front can create pressure and make you lose focus.

▸ *Use verbal or behavioral reminders to direct attention to relevant performance cues:* Whenever your attention starts to drift towards outcomes, do something to get your mind back on track. Use a word, expression, or a gesture that will effectively make you refocus on the cues that are relevant to your performance (refer to Chapter 5 for more on self-talk).

▸ *Keep a positive focus:* A positive focus will prevent you from falling into a negative performance spiral. By choosing to remember your good shots and forgetting about problematic areas, you automatically focus on what you are doing well regardless of the results. For example, if you focus on your great long game even though your putting is making you score badly, you will keep the negativity of the outcome from affecting what you're doing well (your long game).

▸ *Have fun*: Last but not least, have FUN. Remember why you're playing in the first place. Enjoy yourself no matter what happens. Isn't that what golf is all about?

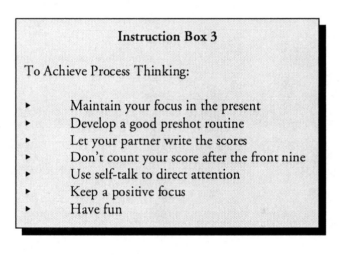

Instruction Box 3

To Achieve Process Thinking:

- ▸ Maintain your focus in the present
- ▸ Develop a good preshot routine
- ▸ Let your partner write the scores
- ▸ Don't count your score after the front nine
- ▸ Use self-talk to direct attention
- ▸ Keep a positive focus
- ▸ Have fun

Hole #4
Self-Beliefs

Par 3

Questions
Never: +2 Sometimes: +1 Always: 0

1- I believe I can become a good golfer.
2- I know I have the necessary skills to shoot low scores.
3- I believe in my abilities to make birdies and pars.

Add 1 stroke to your score
Score:

Self-Beliefs

Beliefs are the guiding light by which we see the world. They filter our perception of reality. Self-beliefs, which are beliefs we hold about ourselves and how we stand in the world, define who we are and how we interpret things that happen to us. In life and in sport, a healthy system of beliefs is essential for success. What we believe about ourselves often become self-fulfilling prophecies.

You may or may not be aware of them, but your beliefs, which are often hidden in your subconscious much like the bulk of an iceberg is hidden under water, guide your performances in profound ways. Beliefs influence self-confidence, motivation, persistence, attributions, expectations, and commitment. If you believe you can't achieve something, you won't be motivated to deploy as much effort as you probably should. Low self-confidence will also result in reduced performance and a tendency to give-up after the first setback. You are also more likely to attribute success to luck or factors outside of your control. However, failures, which are more likely to happen with negative self-beliefs, are attributed to internal factors and reinforce the negative self-belief. In addition, they are also directly responsible for expectations. High expectations can lead to high performance, but low or negative expectations almost always lead to failure.

To illustrate how beliefs influence performance, let's take a look at a classic example: the four-minute mile. Nobody believed the mile could be ran under four minutes before Roger Bannister did it. A wealth of respected medical journals at that time even said that it wasn't humanly possible. Yet, once Bannister tore down the mental barrier, many other people broke the four-minute mile because they now believed that it could be broken.

Just like everyone else, golfers often label themselves as a certain kind of player. It's when these labels are negative or limiting that the troubles start. As a result, they impose limits on themselves that prevent them from achieving their true potential. Your self-beliefs act as a kind of behavioral thermostat that regulates what you can and can't achieve. If you label yourself as a bogey player, and all of a sudden you shoot 40 on the front nine, you think you're playing over your head, and the internal thermostat kicks in. You find yourself playing a horrible back nine to "adjust" your score so that it matches your self-belief. These changes occurred because the belief created anxiety and unwanted pressure as well as distracting thoughts. You think to yourself "Oh my god! I can shoot a great score today" and your focus drifts away from what you were doing so well. As soon as you make a bad shot, you curse yourself instead of accepting the occasional bad shot. "Damn! I just blew it", you say to yourself. This begins a negative cycle that deteriorates performance as you play.

In addition, beliefs are one of the main things guiding selective memory. If you believe you're a slicer, then you'll remember more slices than straight shots. You remember them more because they are *congruent* with your self-beliefs. Your beliefs guide your behaviors, and your behaviors confirm your beliefs. Without knowing it, you find yourself in an insidious failure spiral.

There is good news, however: you have free will. Beliefs are not static, rigid and immutable intellectual concepts. They can be changed. You have the freedom of choice. You can choose to believe whatever you want to believe. You can change these disempowering beliefs and remove the limits you've put on yourself. You are only limited by your own vision.

Exercise 4.1: Changing Negative Self-Beliefs

1. Identify the negative belief

How do you describe or perceive yourself as a golfer? Identify any belief that is detrimental to your game.

2. Choose a positive replacement belief

Once you've identified the disempowering belief, you must choose a replacement belief that will stretch your limits and empower your game. It might be the direct opposite of the negative belief, or it can be something that is beyond, such as "I am a low handicap golfer who can stay in the present and focus on every shot" instead of "I don't have what it takes to shoot low scores". It can even be something that you only want to become. It's always better to have optimistic and empowering beliefs that may not become real than having negative beliefs about yourself that can become real.

3. Choose three or more supporting behaviors

Think of three of more behaviors reflecting this new belief. These behaviors can be based on real memories or imagined, such as a great drive, a perfect chip, or a masterful recovery shot. It might even be receiving a trophy for winning a tournament.

4. Use imagery to mentally rehearse these new behaviors

Finally, picture these behaviors in your head as vividly as you can. See, hear, and feel yourself achieving whatever you want to achieve. Play every detail of it in your mind, as if you were looking at a video. Try to imagine as many details as possible, so that the imagined behaviors/events seem as vivid as the real thing. Then, jump inside yourself and see it through your own eyes as if you were actually there. Experience all the sensations and emotions that are associated with them. Mentally rehearse these behaviors as often as you can so that they are firmly anchored in your mind. In doing so, you create blueprints or memories that will support your new belief. Your brain won't make the difference between a vividly imagined event and an actual event (see Chapter 6 for more details on mental imagery).

Here is a sample of a chart you can fill out to help you change your self-beliefs:

Table 4.1
Sample Self-Belief Chart

Negative or Limiting Self-Belief	Replacement Empowering Self-Belief	Behaviors Supporting New Belief
I can't control my temper	I can control my temper	- Refocusing after a few bad shots - Smile after a missed three-footer - relaxed and cheerful talk
I am a horrible sand player	I can make good bunker shots if I concentrate	- holing a sand shot - getting up & down every time - hitting the pin on the 9th hole
I don't have any talent	I can become a good player if I work hard at it	- winning a tournament - great putter - perfect 7-iron shot

a similar chart can be found in Appendix A, p. 209

If you apply this technique to all of your negative beliefs, you will free yourself to play better golf by removing mental barriers that prevented you from achieving your true potential. Remember, what your mind can conceive, your body can achieve.

Instruction Box 5

▸ Identify any negative or limiting beliefs
▸ Choose a positive replacement belief for each
▸ Choose at least three supporting behaviors for each belief

Hole #5
Self-Talk

Par 4

Questions
Never: +2 Sometimes: +1 Always: 0

1- I have cue words to direct my attention.
2- I can stop negative self-talk.
3- I encourage myself with positive statements.
4- I say positive things to myself after a bad shot.

Add 2 strokes to your score
Score:

Self-Talk

Self-talk is the dialogue that you hold with yourself on and off the golf course. Anytime you are thinking about something, you are in a sense talking to yourself. Most of the time, we are not aware of what we say to ourselves. We continually talk to ourselves in either positive or negative terms which affect our self-confidence, self-image, self-belief, and concentration.

A fine skill such as the golf swing can be influenced by thoughts just prior to its execution. The problem is that most of the time, what we say to ourselves tends to be negative. And on the golf course, negative self-talk becomes a plague that can ruin your game. Saying to yourself "don't put it in the woods", "can't you hit the ball straight for once in your life?", or "you're the worst player" will only hurt your confidence and take away the fun.

Self-talk can be either encouraging or detrimental to your game. That's why it's important to monitor your inner dialogue because what you say to yourself can be self-destructive. We've all had moments where we've berated ourselves after a bad shot. It's easy to come down on yourself when things don't go your way. Even a great player such as Tiger Woods has been heard saying to himself: "Tiger, you're the worst player in the world". Even for the best golfers, negative thinking will often lead to negative performances. That's why the pros try to keep their self-talk positive and encouraging in order to play well.

In sum, self-talk is the key to control your thoughts and emotions. You have the choice: continue to limit yourself with negative self-talk, or stretch your limits and play up to your potential by using positive self-talk. Changing negative self-talk patterns that have been around for years might not be easy. But remember, even thought you cannot always prevent negative thoughts from intruding your consciousness, you can always control the last thought that goes through your mind.

What can self-talk be used for?

▸   *Skill acquisition and refinement:* Self-talk is used by most people when it comes time to learning swing fundamentals. To be able to learn how to swing, we use self-talk to remind ourselves of the basic positions our hands, hips, shoulders, feet, and club have to be in during each step of the swing. While this may be necessary in the beginning, verbal instructions of technical nature are too cumbersome for a skill as complex and brief as the golf swing. Thus, self-talk can be used to break down technical sequences into key words that encompass the whole swing. As your golf swing becomes more automatic, you may want to shift self-talk away from technical reminders to words that direct attention to a certain feel or state of mind. The goal of all golfer should be to promote the automatic execution of the swing.

▸   *Changing bad habits:* Bad habits can be hard to change, especially after years of reinforcement. Self-talk can be used to consciously change bad habits that have become automatic in a golf swing. However, it is essential that what you say to yourself should be focused on what to do instead of what not to do. Cue words can be used to direct attention to the desired changes.

▸   *Attentional control:* Self-talk can be used to redirect your focus to the present if your thoughts drift to the future or dwell on the past. Verbal cues can direct attention to the task at hand and on cues that are critical to the correct execution of a golf swing.

▸   *Creating and changing mood:* Each word has an affective content associated with it. Thus, certain words can be used to create a desired mood. For example, words such as "relax", "smooth", "easy", will create feelings of calmness and control, whereas words such as "power" and "blast" suggest strength and aggressiveness. Golfers can use words such as "come on!", "get a grip", or "you can do it!" to pick themselves up after a bad shot or get pumped up when they are feeling down. The use of the right words can help you control your emotions and lead you to peak performance.

▸ *Controlling effort*: Self-talk can be effective in maintaining energy and persistence. When you get tired at the end of a round or if you are playing in extreme weather conditions, self-talk can be used to remind you how important it is to sustain your efforts despite your fatigue, boredom, or desperation. Appropriate words can renew your commitment to persist in the face of adversity.

▸ *Building self-confidence*: Positive affirmations can be used to increase feelings of confidence and control. Through self-talk, you can encourage and condition yourself for positive thinking that builds self-esteem and confidence (refer to Chapter 7 for more on confidence-building).

Summary Box 5.1

Self-talk can be used to:
- Increase confidence
- Control your mood
- Refocus
- Direct your attention
- Control effort
- Change bad habits
- Acquire & refine skills

Swing keys

Swing keys are another form of self-talk that will help you with your technique by telling you what to focus on during your swing. Swing keys or swing thoughts are the small words that you think about as you are swinging. Most people already have swing thoughts that they use for every swing, but a good swing thought should cover the whole swing as much as possible and stay away from swing mechanics. "Smooth and easy" or "low and away" are good swing thoughts, not "keep your left arm straight" or "keep your right elbow in on the downswing". Swing thoughts, if well trained and rehearsed, can embody a wealth of technical information that would be too cumbersome to go through before a swing. Each swing thought is like the command line or the name of program. On the outside, the process is simple. You just call up the program with a verbal cue and your body automatically executes the technical aspects of the desired swing.

Build a repertoire of swing thoughts for any given shot or to solve any potential swing problems. A particular swing thought might not work on a given day, so start writing down a list of all the ones that worked in the past. Stockpile good swing thoughts, but be careful not to have too many. You might have to change them from day to day or even during a round, but try to keep your swing thoughts as constant as possible to avoid overload.

During the warm-up, assess the kind of swing you've brought to the course so that you can then adjust your swing simply by using the appropriate swing thought.

By rehearsing and practising you swing thoughts and associating them with technical aspects of your swing, you create verbal cues or triggers which activate the desired swing. By doing this, you can make adjustments to your swing on the golf course without ever thinking about mechanics.

How do I improve my self-talk?

1. Awareness
After your round, think about some of the things you said to

yourself. Try to remember the words that you used, and in what situations, then write them down. Awareness is the first step to improvement. Carefully review what you say to yourself in different situations. What kind of thoughts help, what thoughts are harmful, when does a certain kind of self-talk emerge, in what situations are they present?

You can also use imagery to assist you in discovering thought patterns during best and worst performances. Another tool you can use is a self-talk log. Keep a personal log of what you say to yourself, in what circumstances, when they tend to occur, and what are their effects. Write this information down after practice as well as after a round or competition. Below is an example of a self-talk log.

Table 5.1
Sample Self-Talk Log

Self-talk Statements	When	Why	Consequences
I hope I don't make a fool out of myself	first tee	people are watching	I hit a bad shot
Don't hit it fat	after a few fat shots	afraid it will happen again	I skulled the ball
put it in the hole	on the par 3 16th	It was a straight "makable" putt for birdie	a very close miss, but stroke was good
don't three-putt	14th, after 2 consecutive double-bogeys	didn't want to go too far off the hole because would have to putt downhill after	left putt way short and three-putted
I can make this	chip from fringe on 8th	was feeling confident about chipping ability	holed the chip
just relax and concentrate on your shot	on par 3 6th	people were watching	hit a good tee shot
kill this one	tee shot, par 5 17th	reachable par 5, drive was in a groove	crushed it down the middle of the fairway
don't worry about the water	during back-swing on 2nd shot at 4th	water hazard on right and iron swing still shaky	hit the shot fat

a blank copy of this form can be found in Appendix A, p.211

You'll see that as you do this, you'll develop a better awareness of what you say to yourself. The next time you face a difficult shot, stay positive and tell yourself you can make it. Reducing negative self-talk will go a long way to improving your game.

2. Thought-stopping

You can stop negative self-talk by using a trigger to stop the undesirable thought. You can use the word "stop" or a physical action such as clenching your fists, shaking your head, or snapping your fingers. Some people like to imagine a big stop sign or a traffic light. Whatever the trigger, use one that feels natural to you. To be effective, thought-stopping must first be done in practice each time you are aware of negative thoughts. Thought-stopping works best when combined with a physical trigger or with imagery. It will take time, patience, and commitment to be able to use this technique effectively, but it does work in breaking the chain of negative thought patterns.

3. Changing negative self-talk

It may not always be possible to stop negative thoughts when you don't have anything else to think about. Thus, you must reframe these negative thoughts and replace them with positive statements. Try to look at things from a different perspective. Things are only what you make of them, so try to interpret them in a more positive way. For example, instead of saying "I am anxious on the first tee", tell yourself "I am excited on the first tee". Argue against the irrational negative thought. Build a case to refute the underlying assumptions that lead to negativity.

Once you've identified negative self-talk with the help of your self-talk log, you can start reframing or replacing them with more positive statements. If you can't control negative thoughts from coming, at least control the last thought that goes through your mind. Take a deep breath, then repeat the substitute positive affirmation. Below is an example of a chart you can use to change negative self-statements. Remember, to be able to use them effectively on the course, you must have practiced and rehearsed these replacement statements.

Table 5.2
Sample Chart for Self-Talk Change

Negative Self-Talk Statements	Positive Self-Talk Statements
What a lousy warm-up! I can't hit anything today.	It's OK. A warm-up doesn't make a round. You've gotten the bad shots out of your system.
It's too windy	I've played well in windy conditions before.
Why am I so nervous?	Nervousness means you're where you want to be. Get those butterflies in formation!
Don't leave it short	Go for the hole. This one's going in.
You idiot! I can't believe I hit that shot.	It's OK to make a mistake sometimes. The next shot is the one that counts.
What a choker!	You still made par. At least you gave yourself a chance for birdie.

Exercise 5.1: Changing Negative Self-Talk

Think about what you usually say to yourself and fill out a chart similar to the one above (Appendix A, p. 213).

4. Set some goals
With each subsequent round, make it a goal to reduce the prevalence of negative statements by replacing them with positive ones. You can use the following technique to help you achieve your goals.

1.   Put a handful of paper clips in your left pant pocket
2.   Every time you become aware of negative self-talk, simply transfer one paper clip from your left pocket to the right pocket.
3.   At the end of the round, count the number of paper clips in your right pocket and write this number down next to your score.
4.   Set some clear goals for reducing self-talk during rounds. With each round, try to reduce the amount of paper clips in your right pocket.

Self-Talk

Don't be afraid of carrying those paper clips with you to the driving range. People might look at you strangely, but tell yourself that the benefits to your game will surely outweigh a little awkwardness. With commitment and practice, you soon won't need to carry them with you anymore. In the meantime, don't worry about the jingle in your pocket.

Instruction Box 5

- ►   Write down self-statements after each round
- ►   Practice though-stopping
- ►   Change negative to positive self-talk
- ►   Set self-talk goals

Hole #6
Mental Imagery

Par 4

Questions
Never: +2 Sometimes: +1 Always: 0

1- I can visualize my putting line.
2- I know I have the necessary skills to shoot low scores.
3- I mentally replay my best shots before hitting.
4- I can easily see or feel myself executing a perfect shot.

Add 2 strokes to your score
Score:

Mental Imagery

Mental imagery is one of the most effective and proven techniques to enhance performance. Imagery is the sights, sounds, feelings, and smells that we experience in our minds. It involves all of our senses and is like our inner reality. Through imagery, we can create or recreate our own experiences.

All of us already make extensive use of imagery, although we may not call it such or use it systematically. The dream is the best and most salient example of mental imagery. In addition, when we think about what we did during the day, we often use imagery as we try to remember events by re-experiencing them in our minds. Similarly, we rely on imagery when trying to remember someone's face or the location of an object in a room. Thus, most of us have fairly developed abilities to visualize, feel, or hear events in our minds. But to be truly effective, imagery needs to be systematic, controlled, and vivid. Fortunately, imagery skills can be developed, but they need to be practiced regularly to be effective.

Research indicates that the brain does not make any difference between reality and a vividly imagined event. For this reason, elite athletes have made extensive use of imagery to enhance performance. The power of imagery allows athletes to practice sport skills and strategies without physically being in the practice environment. The more skillful they are, the more useful imagery can be for them.

There can be two perspectives in imagery: external and internal. External imagery is when we see ourselves from an external perspective, as if we were looking at a video of ourselves. It is more visual in nature and is very effective for beginners. It is also often used to learn new skills. For golf, external imagery is good when learning swing fundamentals. On the other hand, internal imagery is when we see things through our own eyes, as if we were there. It is more kinesthetic in nature and is more recommended because it has proven more effective in enhancing performance. Internal imagery is often poly-sensory and can trigger strong physiological responses.

A lot of professional golfers, past and present, have used imagery to improve their game. Sam Snead, one of the most successful golfers of all time, would use imagery in three ways:

(1) He would picture the course where he was going to play and the shots he would hit.
(2) He would visualize his swing and, if there was a problem, fix it by seeing it better.
(3) He would see and feel every shot he wanted to hit.

Jack Nicklaus, another golfing legend, talks about "going to the movies" before each shot. Nicklaus would first try to get a feel and picture of his swing, then visualize the flight path of the ball, and finally see it land in the target area. Other golfers such as Davis Love III, Tom Lehman, Fred Couples, Nick Price, and Tom Kite have talked about their use of imagery. The late Harvey Penick, perhaps the greatest teacher of the game, strongly emphasized the importance of imagery in his teaching approach, although he didn't exactly put it in those terms.

Most golfers have experienced some form of involuntary imagery on the golf course. The problem is that most of the time, these images are negative. We've all had flashes of disaster as we were about to hit the ball. Most of the time, the results are similar to the images that flashed through our minds. Negative images can ruin technically sound swings and shatter your confidence. They also create anxiety and distraction from the task at hand. Thus, you must develop strong imagery skills and make systematic use of positive images, sounds, and feelings, if you are to perform to the maximum of your abilities.

Finally, remember that imagery isn't meant to replace physical practice, but it is better than no practice at all. When used in conjunction with physical practice, imagery can be a powerful tool to enhance performance. It takes time and commitment to develop strong imagery skills, but the results are well worth it. Of course, positive imagery doesn't always guarantee positive results, but negative imagery will almost always produce negative results.

Why is imagery effective?

▸ Imagery causes micro-activation in the same muscles that are used during physical movement. With imagery, we can reinforce motor circuits in our brain and between our brain and the muscles involved in the skill.

▸ Imagery creates a mental blueprint of the skill and, through repetitive use, reinforces the mental blueprint and makes the skill become more automatic. It is like programming a computer.

▸ Imagery creates response sets. With the use of imagery, we can plan actions in advance. Responses and solutions can be considered cognitively before a physical response is required. By creating a response set, we can generate different alternatives and deal more effectively with different situations.

▸ Imagery allows us to simulate, create, or recreate experiences that can increase confidence and concentration, reduce stress, and increase composure to be in an optimal state of mind.

When can imagery be used?

▸ *Off-season*: For people who can't play golf year-round, the off-season is a great time to work on your imagery skills. Using appropriate imagery can generate a healthy dose of confidence and keep your mind sharp until the season comes.

▸ *Before and after a round/tournament*: You can mentally simulate an entire round of golf the night before, or just a few problematic or key holes. After your round, retrospective imagery can be used to evaluate your performance and how you felt when things went well or not so well. What went through your mind, how did you feel, how did you prepare for certain shots? All these questions can be answered with imagery.

▶ *Between holes*: Use imagery between holes to keep your focus positive. For example, you can elaborate a routine between each hole to mentally replay your good shots before teeing up on the next hole.

▶ *Before and after a shot/putt/chip*: A lot of professional players try to "see" their shot before hitting the ball. Others mentally replay their best shot in similar situations to give themselves added confidence. With imagery, they feel like they are programming their body to execute the shot desired. After a shot, you can use imagery to reinforce positive results or "fix" a badly executed swing to regain confidence and replace the image of a bad shot with a good one.

▶ *Before and during practice*: Imagery can be used in practice to find out what kind of images work best for you. It is also an opportunity to try different things out and reinforce positive imagery so that it can be effective on the course.

▶ *During and after a lesson*: Imagery can be used to assimilate technical swing lessons and feel the desired changes. A good vision and feel of the desired swing is important when trying to learn or refine your swing. Imagery can make the learning process of technique easier and faster.

Summary Box 6.1

Imagery can be used:

▸ During the off-season
▸ Before and after a round
▸ Between holes
▸ Before and after a stroke
▸ Before and during practice
▸ During and after a lesson

Uses of imagery in golf

- *Success Imagery*: Success imagery is primarily used to increase confidence by replay or creation of successful performances. We can replay our best shots in certain situations, or maybe even see ourselves winning a tournament or a trophy. We can even use successes in other fields (work, family, other sports, education).

- *Preparatory Imagery*: Imagery can be used before hitting a shot in order to program our body to execute the swing we want. This kind of imagery can also increase confidence.

- *Kinesthetic Imagery*: This is very effective in the learning and refinement of the golf swing. Kinesthetic imagery focuses on feel and develops a more acute awareness of our body, muscles, and golf club.

- *Simulation*: Simulation allows us to experience all kinds of things without physically being there. We can hit all kinds of shots, play entire rounds or tournaments, or just experience specific situations through simulation. Simulation not only improves concentration, but allows us to cope with potential problems. We can simulate being in a certain situation and reacting in an ideal way. We can learn how to deal with stress, distractions, and negative emotions through simulation. During practice, we can simulate playing an actual round of golf and the pressure and feelings associated with each shot.

- *Learning and refinement of golf swing:* Imagery can be used to learn and internalize swing fundamental or swing changes. We can watch a model execute a perfect golf swing and try to visualize ourselves doing the same swing. Through imagery, we can try to see where mistakes in the swing arise and correct them.

- *Affective Imagery:* We can recreate situations of anxiety, frustration, fear, or pain, and find better ways to react to them. By practising ideal reactions and strategies for each situation through imagery, we will be able to cope better with them.

- *Healing Imagery:* Imagery can significantly increase the healing process of an injury.

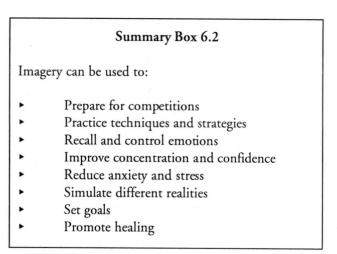

Summary Box 6.2

Imagery can be used to:

- ▸ Prepare for competitions
- ▸ Practice techniques and strategies
- ▸ Recall and control emotions
- ▸ Improve concentration and confidence
- ▸ Reduce anxiety and stress
- ▸ Simulate different realities
- ▸ Set goals
- ▸ Promote healing

How to practice imagery?

1- Imagery is often preceded by a short relaxation session to increase concentration. Find a quiet place where you will not be disturbed, assume a comfortable position and relax completely.

2- If you have never done any imagery training, start with simple and familiar images (workplace, home, golf club). During the first 2 weeks or so, take 5 minutes each day to work on your imagery skills. Try to see and experience as much details as possible.

3- Once you are good at imagining simple images, start increasing the complexity and the duration of your imagery (10-15 minutes). Try to combine all your senses and feel the same physical sensations as if you were actually in the real-life situation.

4- As you develop better imagery skills, try to change the sub-modalities of your images. For example, vary perspectives, sound amplitude, color, lightness, or the contrast of your images. This will help you develop greater control over your imagery.

Finally, some people like to actually move their body as they are imagining a particular movement. This helps develop more kinesthetic awareness and feel in the appropriate muscles.

Remember, imagery is an exercise in concentration, which means that it is demanding. If you are mentally tired, stop. Quality is better than quantity.

Exercises

Here are some exercises that will help you get started on your imagery training:

Exercise 6.1: Place yourself in a familiar place where you usually perform (driving range, golf course). It is empty except for you. Look all around, and notice the quiet emptiness. Pick out as many details as you can. What does it smell like? Now imagine yourself in the same place, but with a lot of people around. Imagine yourself getting ready to hit on the first tee, and see your partners or anybody else that might be around. Try to experience this image from inside your body. Try to hear the sounds associated with this moment, and then imagine the hushed quietness as you are about to hit. Recreate the feeling of nervous anticipation and excitement that you have as you are about to hit this first shot. What is going through your mind as you stand over the ball? Notice the tension in your muscles. Are you relaxed or tense?

Exercise 6.2: Try to imagine the fine details of a golf ball. Turn it over in your hands and examine every part of the ball. Feel its outline and structure. Notice its whiteness, its dimples, even perhaps the scratches on it. Read the logo of the ball company written on its surface. Put the ball on the ground, and notice how it sits on the grass. Try to imagine a glow of color surrounding your ball, as if a strange aura was emanating from it. Imagine taking the club back, and continue seeing how the ball looks like. Try to continue seeing that glow surrounding the ball. Now, imagine the club strike the ball. Hear the contact between the club face and the ball. Watch its flight through the air. What happens to its color? Step outside of your body and see yourself hitting this ball as if you were watching yourself on film. Now, step back in your body and see it through your own eyes. Continue hitting the ball and try to hear, feel, and see everything as if you were there.

Exercise 6.3: Pick a shot (driver, iron, chip, putt) and perform it over and over in your mind. Imagine every feeling and movement in your muscles as you execute the shot. Try to feel this image as if you were inside your own body. Concentrate on how the different parts of your body feel as you stretch and contract the various muscles associated with the shot.

Now, try to combine all your senses, but particularly those of feeling, seeing, and hearing yourself perform the skill over and over. Do not concentrate too hard on any one sense. Instead, try to imagine the total experience using all of your senses.

You can do this with each club in your bag, and even imagine different types of shot (rough, sand, fade, draw, knock-down, etc.) in different situations (competition, after a few bad shots, in the zone, etc.).

Exercise 6.4: Choose a particular shot that you have trouble hitting. Begin practising the shot over and over in your mind. See and feel yourself doing this from inside your body. If you make a mistake or perform the shot incorrectly, stop the image and repeat it, attempting to perform perfectly every time. Recreate past experiences in which you have not hit the shot well. Take careful notice of what you were doing wrong. Now imagine yourself executing the shot correctly. Focus on how your body feels as you go through the different positions.

Exercise 6.5: Think back and choose a past round in which you performed very well. Using all your senses, recreate that round in your mind. See yourself as you were succeeding, hear the sounds involved, feel your body as you perform the movements, and re-experience the positive emotions. Try to pick out the characteristics that made you perform so well (intense concentration, feelings of confidence, etc). After identifying these characteristics, try to determine why they were present during that round. Think about the things you did in preparation for that particular round. What are some things that may have caused this great performance?

Repeat this exercise for a situation in which you performed poorly.

Exercise 6.6: Think back to a situation where you experienced a great deal of anxiety. Recreate that situation in your head, seeing and hearing yourself. Especially recreate that feeling of anxiety. Try to feel the physical responses of your body to the emotion, and also try to recall the thought going through your mind that may have caused this anxiety. Now, attempt to let go of the anxiety and relax your body. Breathe slowly and deeply and focus on your body as you exhale. Imagine all of the tension being pulled into your lungs and exhaled from your body. Continue breathing slowly and exhaling tension until you are deeply relaxed. Try to repeat this exercise for a situation in which you experienced a great deal of anger or frustration.

Exercise 6.7: Imagine yourself making two perfect shots and leaving your ball just three feet from the cup on a par 4. Imagine missing the birdie putt, and try to recreate your deception and frustration. How would you react? Are you thinking about the missed putt or the two perfect shots? If you are thinking about the putt, try to experience the disappointment you would feel if that really happened. Does this affect your mood and do you carry this negative attitude through the next hole? Find a way to forget about this putt, about your anger and frustration, and refocus on the task at hand. Can you make any corrections to your preparation or your stroke if you had a similar putt in the future? Try to find a way to keep your confidence on the greens and refocus. Get ready for your next shot with a confident, calm, and focused attitude.

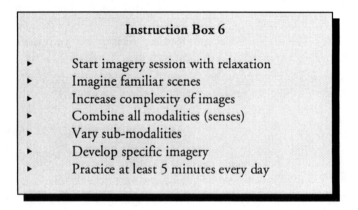

Instruction Box 6

- Start imagery session with relaxation
- Imagine familiar scenes
- Increase complexity of images
- Combine all modalities (senses)
- Vary sub-modalities
- Develop specific imagery
- Practice at least 5 minutes every day

Hole #7
Confidence

Par 4

Questions
Never: 0 Sometimes: +1 Always: +2

1- I loose confidence if I didn't hit well during the warm-up.
2- I think about swing mechanics before hitting.
3- I lose confidence after a bad shot.
4- I don't feel confident before hitting.

Add 2 strokes to your score
Score:

Confidence

Confidence is the cornerstone of performance. In any sports, and especially golf, confidence and belief in one's abilities is crucial to excellence. Lack of confidence causes indecision, self-doubt, anxiousness, and distractive thoughts. Golfers with low self-confidence have trouble staying in the present, are easily distracted from the task at hand, don't trust their swing, and often become too analytical. As a result, their swing becomes tentative and mechanical, and their mind is focused on what not to do instead of what to do. They start thinking about the lake on the right of the green, about the bunkers in front, about what people will think of them if they fail, and so on. Fear of failure instills indecision and doubt, and under these conditions, many people start focusing on mechanical things such as how to turn their hips, transfer their weight, or how to position their arms, wrists and elbows. Instead of focusing on swing mechanics, golfers should let go and play with their eyes, just as they would if they were to throw a ball. In other words, the best course of action is to focus on the target and trust your swing.

It's easy to feel confident when you are playing well, but the challenge is to remain confident even when things go astray. That's the difficult part, one that every golfer continually struggles with. The truth is: confidence is not something divine or mysterious that falls upon us. It can be learned. But it takes commitment to develop confidence.

How can a golfer build unshakable confidence, then? The answer isn't simple, and the solution isn't easy. You will probably lose confidence at one time or another, no matter how well you think. The important thing is to minimize the occurrence and duration of these self-doubt bouts.

Confidence

Use success memories

First of all, a golfer must use success memories instead of failure memories. How often do you step up to a ball, faced with a shot you have missed in the past, and all you can think about is how badly you hit it last time, and how you don't want this to happen again. That's negative thinking, and that kind of thinking can only hurt you. Instead, step up to the ball and replay your best shots in your mind. See them, hear them, feel them. Have a success memory for each type of shot, be it real or not. You can even use non-golf success memories. You must probably excel at something totally unrelated with golf, such as another sport, academics, work, or even cooking. Draw on these memories. Remind yourself how competent you are. This programs your brain to think positively, to instill confidence.

Quality practice

Second, practice both your body and your mind well. Quality practice is purposeful. It involves having a clear goal every time you practice. You can't go to the range and beat ball after ball without any purpose. That's just a waste of time and energy. Practice like you play. If you know that you have practiced well, you will feel confident during a round. You will trust what you have practiced, and your swing will be doubt-free.

Create a good routine

Third, create a good preshot routine that will set you up well before each shot, both physically and mentally. A good routine will serve to empty your mind of distractions and self-doubt, make you focus on the relevant cues critical to performance (e.g., your target), and ensure that you make a decisive shot.

Accept mistakes

Fourth, remember that you are only human, and humans make mistakes. Being a perfectionist will only bring frustration and resentment. We are not perfect, and we can't expect to play perfect golf. Don't forget that failure is a natural part of the road to success. The most important thing is to learn from our mistakes. Every so-called

Confidence

failure is a stepping stone to success.

Positive interpretations
Finally, you create your own reality. Some people might disagree, but reality is subjective. You can choose to think however you want, be it irrational or not, as long as it makes you feel confident. Some people might say that this is self-deception, but what is the alternative? If you do not trust your abilities and think you can achieve success, how are you thinking then? Would being "realistic", which may mean doubting your abilities and bringing yourself down, make you perform better? If you think well, you'll soon find out that you weren't fooling yourself. A wise old monk once said: "Reality is a slave of the mind. The mind shapes it, gives it form. The mind *is* reality". What really matters is how you interpret things, and you have to interpret them in a way that maximizes your confidence.

That's what thinking well means. It means remembering your good shots and forgetting about the bad ones. It means having quality practice and trusting your mind-body connection. It means building a success repertoire and drawing on it in the face of adversity. It means creating a good routine and committing to it. It means taking temporary failure as a stepping stone to future success.

That's what a confident golfer is all about.

Further suggestions for confidence building

▸ Remember your good shots, and forget about the bad ones. Use memories of successful shots each time you step up to the ball. Create or recreate a memory for each type of shot. Try to see, hear, and feel successful shots. You can even use non-golf success memories. Draw on these memories. Remind yourself how competent you are. This programs your brain to think positively, to instill confidence.

▸ Use imagery to review your successful shots or rounds. Try to remember what it felt like, and re-experience the positive feelings they generated. You can also watch actual video footage of yourself performing in a tournament or view a clip of your flawless swing.

▶ Use top golfers as models. Pretend you are Tiger Woods or Jack Nicklaus and model their confident attitude and thought patterns. Imagine how they would react to the situations you are facing. Imitate their behaviors, work ethic, and attitude.

▶ Train your mind and body well. If you know you've practiced with the upmost quality, you'll feel more confident about your abilities. Practice your weaker shots, and make sure your mental preparation is top-notch. You can make use of mental plans such as pre-competition, competition, and refocus plans (refer to Chapters 15 and 16).This kind of preparation can only instill confidence.

▶ Develop a good preshot routine (Chapter 12) that will prevent negative thoughts from entering your mind. You can also develop a good post-shot routine that encourages positive thinking. Good routines improve performance and consistency, which will in turn create feelings of confidence.

▶ Learn from your mistakes. Mistakes or failures are a part of the road to success. We are not perfect, and we can't expect to play perfect golf. Leave perfectionism in the clubhouse. Remember that every so-called failure is a stepping stone to success.

▶ Think positive. The way you interpret what happens to you is more important than what happens to you. Berating yourself won't make you play better. Always think in a way that will maximize your confidence. If you've had a good warm-up, tell yourself that you're ready to play a great round. If you've had a bad warm-up, tell yourself that you've gotten the bad shots out of your system.

▶ Be aware of negative thoughts or self-beliefs (Chapter 4).

Confidence

Replace any negative feelings or thoughts with positive ones (for more information on how to change self-talk, refer to chapter 5).

- Give yourself credit for your achievements. Attribute success to your abilities and your hard work instead of luck. Confident people create their own luck.

- Be aware of your body language. Keep your head up despite adversity. Negative body language often translate automatically to negative feelings, but the same holds true for positive body language. Stand tall with your head up high and shoulders back even if you feel down. With each breath you take, breathe in confidence and breathe out self-doubt.

- Even when you don't feel confident, pretend you are. Act confident, and try to have the same attitude as when you're on top of your game. You have to walk the walk and talk the talk. Soon, you'll see that you'll be walking the talk.

- If you fail to achieve your goals and lose confidence in your abilities as a result, your goals may be too ambitious for your current dispositions. Set new goals or modify existing ones to allow you to realistically achieve them given the time and effort you are willing to put in. If you still want to achieve those same difficult and challenging goals, you may have to review your level of commitment in terms of time and effort. To achieve excellence, sacrifices have to be made. Remember, take it one step at a time. Build on small successes.

Summary Box 7.1

Suggestions for improving confidence:

- Remember good shots and forget bad ones
- Mentally review successful shots
- Model attitude of top golfers
- Quality practice
- Develop a good preshot routine
- Accept and learn from mistakes
- Think positive
- Change self-beliefs and attributions
- Give yourself credit
- Watch out for negative body language
- Pretend you're confident
- Review your goals

Exercise 7.1: Positive Affirmation List

Develop a list of positive affirmations. Creating such a list will help you overcome the habit of negative thinking and self-doubt, which will result in negative self-beliefs.

- Start with 5 to 10 positive statements related to the qualities you have or would like to have in golf. This list is for your eyes only and should contain statements that have personal meaning to you.

- Have this list in a place that is readily visible every day. Examples of such places might be beside the phone, on your bedroom door, or next to the mirror.

- Repeat these self-affirming statements every day.

▶ Repeat these affirmations each time you are at the driving range or during a round.

Finally, feel free to add new affirmations or modify existing ones every now and then, and repeat them every day even though you already feel confident. Here is a sample of such a list:

Table 7.1
Sample of Positive Affirmations List

LIST OF PERSONAL AFFIRMATIONS
I am confident in my technical abilities
I can stay focused under pressure
I am mentally tough
I can come back stronger after a mistake
I have a great short game

a blank form similar to this one can be found in Appendix A, p.215

In addition to this list, you can also create a list of personal achievements reminders. This list contains affirmations referring to your personal successes in golf, but can also reflect success in other fields as well. The list should contain events of achievements that you are personally proud of and that are gratifying to you. Just like in the previous list, don't be modest. Be boastful and make yourself look good. To produce a strong sense of confidence and self-belief, you can't be afraid to be a little arrogant. You can repeat the same 4 steps outlined for the list of personal affirmations, but you might also want to keep this list for times of greater need such as after a failure. Finally, don't hesitate to continually update this list with new achievements.

Exercise 7.2: List of Personal Achievements

Develop a personal achievement list such as the one below.

Table 7.2
Personal Achievement List

LIST OF PERSONAL ACHIEVEMENTS
I blew away everybody at this tournament last year
I played my best round after a horrible start last week
I played extremely well in windy conditions so far
I got promoted last month because of my good work
I am ranked in the top 5 in my country

a blank form similar to this one can be found in Appendix A, p.217

You can create small cards containing positive statements about yourself and carry them with you on the golf course. Read them before your round or each time you are waiting to hit a shot.

Instruction Box 7

- Keep your thoughts and attitude positive
- Use positive memories
- Train well
- Develop confidence-building strategies
- Act confident

Hole #8
Composure

Par 5

Questions
Never: 0 Sometimes: +1 Always: +2

1- I have trouble sinking pressure putts.
2- I am anxious when there is water or sand nearby.
3- I get frustrated when plays slows down.
4- I get angry after a bad shot.
5- Once I get angry or frustrated, I find it hard to regain control of my game.

Add 2 strokes to your score
Score:

Composure

Being able to keep your composure in critical situations or after a mistake is critical to success. Bobby Jones, who is the only golfer in history to win the Grand Slam, didn't started winning consistently before he was able to control his temper. When we talk about composure, we have to take two things into consideration: anxiety (stress), and physical intensity (body activation). We perform our best with a certain level of anxiety and intensity. This range of anxiety/intensity where peak performance can occur is called the Zone of Optimal Functioning (ZOF). This zone is different for each individual and each sport. For example, a weight-lifter needs a high level of intensity to perform best, but this same level of intensity would be detrimental to a golfer's performance.

Mental anxiety, which results from worry, fear, doubt, and indecision, must usually be kept at a minimal level for peak performance to occur. Physical intensity, however is more relative. While you need a certain level of activation, too much intensity can disrupt the fine skills involved in a golf swing and adversely affect performance. You have to find that right balance of activation and relaxation, sort of an even keel. Sam Snead uses the expression "cool-mad" to help him find that right balance.

In golf, pressure situations as well as frustrating moments are abundant. If you cannot stay composed through these moments, you won't be able to play your best golf. Therefore, it is important to know how to find your personal ZOF, recognize your current intensity/anxiety level, and adjust them within your ZOF if necessary.

What is the relation between intensity and performance?

High anxiety usually results in high intensity, but high intensity will not necessarily result in high anxiety. A high level of physical activation (intensity), which could be the result of anger and frustration, will cause muscle tension and physical symptoms such as an elevated heartbeat, sweaty palms, and tremors. Excess muscle tension can disrupt your golf swing or your putting stroke. Ever noticed that you don't hit as hard when you try to kill it? Excess muscle tension causes your movements to become jerky and might result in less distance and accuracy. In addition, high physical intensity lowers kinesthetic awareness, which means that you loose feel. In golf, feel is very important, especially for the short game.

What is the relation between anxiety and performance?

Anxiety originating from fear, worry, doubt, or indecision are usually a source of distraction by diverting your focus away from task-relevant cues. If you are worried about missing a shot, you are not focused on making the shot. In addition, high anxiety almost always creates high physical activation. As we have seen, too much intensity will result in muscle tension, which will hurt the fluidity and smoothness of your swing. However, if you have learned to cope with anxiety, you can prevent muscle tension as well as stay focus on task-relevant cues. Sometimes, anxiety or stress is unconscious and inevitable, but it can be used to your advantage. It's not a question of eliminating the butterflies in your stomach, it's a question of getting them to fly in formation. In the following pages, you will learn how to cope with pressure and use your emotions to your advantage.

How do I find my ZOF?

Finding your optimal level of intensity is a question of experience. The ZOF only exists in your mind. It is subjective. Thus, you must pay attention to how you are feeling and rate that intensity according to your own criteria. Once you've subjectively differentiated between different levels of intensity, you must associate them with your performance. Did a certain level of intensity produce good or bad performances? What was your intensity level during your best

Composure

performance? Were you relaxed or highly charged? Finding your ZOF is not an easy task. You must constantly monitor yourself and learn from each experience. Pay careful attention to how you were feeling before each round or competition. Examine your best and worst performances (see Chapter 1).

Adjusting intensity in the ZOF

Once you know what level of physical activation is needed, you must do frequent intensity checks before and during a round to adjust it if necessary. Understand when and why you tend to be over-active or flat, and include intensity checks at those critical moments in your game plan.

Strategies to adjust intensity:

Psyching-up strategies (intensity increase)

► Inspirational music: Music can be very effective for a pre-competition pump up. The type of music chosen is very personal, but there have been certain favorites that athletes often use. Themes from sport movies such as "Rocky" are very popular. Other upbeat and meaningful songs such as "Simply the best" from Tina Turner or "We are the champions" from Queen are also very effective. If you tend to feel tired and flat in the morning, then play an energizing song in the car on your way over to the golf course.

► Physical exertion: Physical exercise is still one of the best methods to pump up. Running a few short sprints, jumping jacks, or any other vigorous physical activity can get your heart rate up and increase respiration. If you're on the golf course and need to energize yourself, walk faster between each shot and allow yourself to express your emotions (good or bad), as long as you remain in control.

▸ Breathing: Simply increasing your respiratory rate can make you feel more active and energized. With each inhalation, imagine yourself generating more energy while dumping away fatigue with each exhalation.

▸ Imagery: The use of energizing images can be effective to charge you up. Develop a bank of images to be used in various situations and practice using these cues to energize.

▸ Self-talk: Verbal expressions such as "go!", "let's do it!", "explode!" can serve as effective activating cues. Know what type of thoughts/words are effective to energize you and practice them regularly. Self-talk can even more effective if combined with imagery.

Summary Box 8.1

Psyching-up strategies:

▸ Inspirational music
▸ Physical activity
▸ Faster breathing
▸ Energetic imagery
▸ Self-talk

Strategies to decrease physical activation

▸ Slowing down: If you need to remain calm and decrease physical activation, then walking more slowly or just slowing everything down can be effective. Take your time between each shot.

▸ Deep breathing: Relaxation exercises will be covered more

thoroughly at the end of this chapter, but there is a simple breathing method you can use to decrease physical activation. Take deep breaths from you abdomen, slowly filling your lungs from the bottom up by pushing your abdomen out. Continue by expanding the chest and slightly lift your shoulders until your lungs are full, then slowly exhale by pulling the abdomen in and lowering your chest. As you exhale, tell yourself: "relax". Practice taking 30 or 40 deep breaths each day, associating it with the relaxed feeling in your body.

Summary Box 8.2

Strategies to decrease intensity:

▸   Slowing down
▸   Relaxation

Dealing with anxiety and competitive pressure

Bad performances are often the result of excessive fear, worry, or doubt. Cognitive anxiety will also result in muscle tension and fatigue. You cannot perform at your best when you are uptight. It's therefore important to understand your own patterns of stress and manage them before they get out of control. If you allow anxiety to become too great, then you might suffer a catastrophic drop in performance (or choke). By that time, it will be too late to recover. Hence, the most important thing about anxiety is to recognize and adjust it before it gets out of hand.

Strategies to adjust anxiety

▸   Changing appraisal: High anxiety is often caused by the distorted way we perceive reality. Fear of failure, worry about the demands of the situation, and doubting your ability to cope with the demands can cause a great deal of anxiety and stress. Instead of fear, worry, and doubt, replace these irrational beliefs with more constructive thoughts. Instead of saying to yourself "I can't make this putt", tell yourself "It's a tough putt, but I can sink it". Challenge yourself to make good shots every time you're under pressure.

▸ Keeping things in perspective: Things are only what you make of them. You don't need to play perfect golf to win. You don't need to drive it 300 yards down the middle each time. You don't have to make every three-footer. You don't have to chip it inside two feet every time. You are human, and part of being human is about making mistakes. Perfectionism leads nowhere. The world won't stop turning if you fail. No shot is a matter of life and death. All you can do is try your best, then accept the results. Sure it's important, but it's also only a game.

▸ Re-framing feelings: When you start feeling nervous, don't start to wonder what is wrong with you. Being nervous doesn't hurt your performance as much as it takes your attention away from the present. It's normal to be a little stressed in pressure situations, but use it to your advantage instead of turning it against yourself. Tell yourself that if you're a little nervous, it's because this is where you want to be. If you didn't play well, how can you get a birdie opportunity or have the chance to win the tournament? Learn to love pressure.

▸ Imagery: Imagery, combined with self-talk, can be a very powerful tool to reduce mental anxiety. Do some positive imagery every time you feel stressed. Recall past successes and remind yourself how good you are. Recall everything about a previous successful performance and use it as a reminder of your abilities. If you've done it once, you can do it again.

Summary Box 8.3

Strategies to adjust anxiety:

▸　Changing appraisal
▸　Keeping things in perspective
▸　Reframing feelings
▸　Imagery
▸　Relaxation

Relaxation to decrease intensity and anxiety

Relaxation can be useful to decrease both physical intensity and mental anxiety before, during, and after a round of golf. Relaxation allows you to clear your mind and conserve precious physical and mental energy. It prepares the mind and body for quality performance and speeds up recovery. Furthermore, knowing how to relax can facilitate deep and restful sleep, especially before an important competition. There are many relaxation techniques available, but the one that probably works best for you is one that is personal. Think of existing strategies that you use to relax. What can calm you down? For some people, it's imagining themselves on a warm and sandy beach, listening to the waves. For others, it's listening to the gentle sounds of a stream. Imagining yourself in a calm outdoor setting can be very effective to induce a relaxation response. Other things such as taking a warm bath, talking to friends, listening to music, or reading, can be very effective relaxing activities. Again, the only rule is what works for you.

However, while there are many different natural ways to relax outside of the competitive environment, relaxing under the pressure of a round is a little harder and requires more work. You need to be able to relax quickly during a round in order to keep your composure. Thus, relaxation strategies need to be practiced extensively under low-stress situations before they can be effective under high stress. It's when you're angry about missing five shots in a row or when you're putting for the championship that you need to relax the most. You need to induce a relaxation response between each shot or in the space of one deep breath just before making a shot. To be able to do this, you need to practice. Whatever relaxation strategy or technique you use, you need to recognize the difference between anxiety and the feeling of relaxation. It's also useful to associate the relaxed state with a cue (word, phrase, or physical trigger) to be able to recall it when desired without having to go through a lengthy relaxation procedure.

Relaxation Exercises

A few of the more popular relaxation exercises are presented in this section. Choose whatever method you like best, but always practice in a calm, quiet environment first before attempting to do it in competition.

Remember, these relaxation exercise have to be practiced frequently. Set a goal to relax a certain amount of time each day. You can do this anywhere. At home, at work, at school, or at practice. Use every stressful event as an opportunity to practice your relaxation strategies, and always remember to associate a trigger to the state of relaxation.

Progressive Relaxation

This relaxation method consists of successively contracting and relaxing specific muscles groups for several seconds. The succession of contractions and relaxations in each muscle group serves to gain greater awareness on the difference between muscular tension and relaxation. The exercise progresses through each muscle group, generally from the legs up, until all the major muscles in the body are relaxed. Some people like to start from the legs and move up, while others like to start from the head and move down (forehead, eyebrows, jaws, lips, neck, shoulders, upper arms, forearms, wrists, hands, fingers, chest, abdomen, back, buttocks, thighs, calves, ankles, feet and toes). Use whatever sequence you prefer, but relax one muscle group at a time. A feeling of warmth and heaviness generally accompanies the relaxation response. Small twitches and spasms can also be expected if there is a lot of muscle tension.

Progressive relaxation can either be done in a sitting or lying position and is useful before going to sleep or after a hard workout. The goal of this exercise is to teach you what relaxed muscles feel like in order to be able to induce a relaxation response in an instant.

Start by contracting each muscle group for about 10 to 15 seconds, followed by a 15 to 20-second release. Work you way through each muscle group until your whole body is relaxed. As you get better at it, you can decrease the contraction time or eliminate it completely. A full script for this relaxation method can be found in Appendix B.

Deep Breathing

This is the easiest and fastest way to relax. It also facilitates oxygen intake and waste removal. Most people are shallow chest breathers and don't really promote good air circulation in their lungs. As a result, tension and fatigue set in and impair performance.

Proper breathing occurs when the diaphragm moves down and pushes the abdomen out. The vacuum created sucks air into the lower parts of the lungs. The middle and upper portions of the lungs are then filled by raising the chest and shoulders. Inhalation should be continuous and transition should be smooth between each stage. To exhale, pull the abdomen in to force the air out, then lower the chest and shoulders to empty the lungs. While you are exhaling, repeat to yourself: "relax". Feel the tension leave your body as you exhale.

Take about 30 or 40 deep breaths each day, and associate the relaxed state with a cue word. Each time you are stressed, take a deep breath and let go of the tension. Once you become good at relaxing under stressful conditions, incorporate a deep breath into your preshot routine (Chapter 12).

Composure

Meditation

Meditation can help you induce a state of deep relaxation and help with concentration. When practising meditation, it's important to be in a quiet environment and be in a comfortable position. It's also necessary to adopt a passive attitude and focus attention on a single thought, sound, or object. The most common mental device used in meditation is the repetition of a mantra, a meaningless rhythmic sound of one or two syllables (e.g., "ahhom").

To be able to meditate, it's important not to try too hard and just let it happen. You must quiet your logical and analytical mind and let your mind go blank. Be patient, and when your thoughts start to wander, gently bring attention back to your mantra (or any other mental device used). Be passive and let thoughts flow through consciousness without attending to them.

In sum, to meditate, first find a quiet place to sit. Close your eyes and relax all your muscles. Breathe calmly through the nose, concentrating on the rhythm of your respiration. Focus on one single cue (mantra) and continue to breathe regularly. Don't worry if you can't relax right away. Just keep breathing regularly and focus on your mantra. Practice every day for about 10 to 15 minutes. Regular meditation will keep your mind fresh and your body alert.

Autogenic Training

Autogenic training is similar to auto-hypnosis and involves feelings of warmth and heaviness in the limbs. Start by concentrating on feelings of heaviness in your arms, moving from the dominant to the non-dominant arm. You can flex your arms and move your body to help you get the sensation of heaviness. Spend about one minute on each arm, then move to the legs in the same sequence (dominant followed by non-dominant). Breathe regularly and keep a passive attitude throughout the session. Once a sense of heaviness is produced, you can move to the next stage of training. Repeat the same procedure for warmth. Focus on the sensation of warmth while repeating to yourself three to five times how warm your limb is.

Once you have mastered feelings of heaviness and warmth, it's time to regulate heartbeat. Repeat to yourself: "my heartbeat is calm and regular" three to five times during a minute. Take a small break, then do it again. Do this four times.

Now that your heartbeat is regular and calm, concentrate on your breathing rate and repeat the same procedure done previously for heartbeat. Repeat the same procedure for the next two stages, which involve warmth in the solar plexus area and coolness on the forehead, respectively.

As you become proficient, you can go through all six stages (heaviness, warmth, heartbeat, breathing, warmth in solar plexus, coolness on forehead) in a matter of minutes. You can then combine the initial six stages with imagery to produce a deeper relaxation state. Your imagery can be some relaxing scene or specific themes such as being in the "zone" or winning.

Autogenic training may take several weeks or months, and once it has been mastered, you can induce it very quickly and sustain a relaxation response for 30 minutes to an hour.

Summary Box 8.4

Relaxation exercises:

- ▸ Progressive relaxation
- ▸ Deep breathing
- ▸ Meditation
- ▸ Autogenic training

Instruction Box 8

- Find ZOF
- Learn how to increase intensity
- Learn how to lower intensity
- Learn how to decrease anxiety
- Experiment with different relaxation exercises

Hole #9
Concentration

Par 5

Questions
Never: 0 Sometimes: +1 Always: +2

1- I get distracted when there are people watching.
2- I let my daily hassles affect my game on the course.
3- I think about past mistakes or have difficulty forgetting them.
4- I think about the consequences of making or missing a shot.
5- I get distracted when the group behind is catching up.

Add 2 strokes to your score
Score:

Concentration

Concentration is perhaps the most important determinant in a successful golf shot. Most players are distracted or not totally concentrated on their shot at one time or another. Each time this happens, you can lose a stroke or two. If this happens only 4 or 5 times a round, it could add a lot of strokes to your score. Thus, with so little time spent on actually executing a shot, concentration is crucial to golfing success. Fortunately, the ability to concentrate is a skill that can be developed and improved through practice.

How do you improve concentration? Teachers in every discipline expect students to have better concentration simply by asking them to concentrate more. In reality, you can't improve concentration by telling yourself to "concentrate" if you've never learned how. Concentration has many components, the first of which is attention. There are four different types of attentional focus or style. Attentional style refers to the manner in which you direct your attention on a given task. Researchers have classified these styles along two dimensions: width and direction. The width dimension of an athlete's attentional focus ranges from broad to narrow, while the direction dimension varies from internal to external. An external focus requires an athlete to attend to people, events, or objects in the external environment, while an internal focus is directed to the athlete's thoughts, emotions, and physical status. Broad and narrow attentional focus allows one to attend to many or just one cue.

Having good concentration involves achieving the following skills:

Matching Attentional Demands

Each of us has a dominant attentional style that is relatively stable across situations. This style determines how you focus your attention in a given situation and may or may not be suitable to the demands of the activity in which you are engaged in. For example, hitting a golf ball requires a narrow-external focus. When your attentional style matches the demands of the activity, performance will be facilitated. Thus, if your attentional style tends to be narrow and external, you'll have a focus that will be more helpful to a successful shot. If, however, your attentional style is broad and internal when you are about to swing, then you allow too many distracting thoughts into your mind and performance will likely be poor because you are not attending to task-relevant cues.

Fortunately, your attentional focus is not static. It will vary along the two dimensions (broad-narrow, internal-external) across different activities and even within an activity. This brings us to another crucial element of attention: the ability to shift attention.

Shifting Attention

In golf, you need to shift your attention many times over the course of a round. You need to have a broad-external focus before executing a shot to take into account information such as hazards and course conditions. Once this assessment is complete, attentional focus must be broad-internal to allow you to plan your shot. Information such as past experiences, tactical situation, and current quality of play determine club selection and the type of shot to be hit. Then, you need to shift to a narrow-internal focus to monitor your own tension and mentally rehearse the shot. Finally, attentional focus becomes narrow-external as you start your back-swing and hit the ball.

Optimizing Intensity

Intensity, or physical activation, has a direct effect on your focus of attention. When intensity is too high, your attentional focus narrows and you have what might be called "tunnel vision". In team sports such as hockey and football, having a narrow focus of attention is often detrimental to performance. But in golf, a narrow focus of attention is appropriate. The problem, however, is that high intensity also creates muscle tension, which will adversely affect a fine motor skill such as the golf swing. Thus, it is better to keep physical activation at an appropriate and comfortable level (for more information on intensity, see Chapter 8).

Blocking Distractions

Because we have limited information processing capacity, we need to be able to attend only to the cues that are critical to performance and block out irrelevant stimuli. Thus, knowing what cues to focus on and keeping your focus on those cues is critical to performance. Distraction control will be discussed in greater detail later in this chapter.

Controlling your Thoughts

Concentration also involves the ability to control our thought processes. This means that you should think in a way that allows you to maintain and optimize your concentration. Knowing what you need to focus on to play well as well as potential distractors can help you concentrate better. Process thinking is more helpful than outcome thinking and will help you to concentrate on appropriate performance cues instead of wasting precious mental energy on uncontrollable factors (see Chapter 3).

Furthermore, confidence affects concentration, which means that you must nurture thoughts that promote confidence. As we have seen, there are many ways of thinking that can help you build confidence (see Chapter 7).

Positive focusing is important because negative thoughts often cause distraction from the cues you need to focus on for a good shot execution. Negative thoughts often cause people to become too analytical also. When you're playing golf, you want to keep things simple and not analyze too much to avoid mental overload or paralysis by analysis.

Hence, keeping your thoughts and your self-talk positive can enhance concentration by affecting confidence and anxiety, which are directly related to your ability to concentrate.

Refocusing when Distracted

    The final component in concentration is your ability to refocus in the face of distractions. Although you may minimize the chances of it happening, sometimes distractions are inevitable. Thus, the ability to refocus is an essential component of concentration. Refocusing strategies will be discussed in greater detail later in this chapter.

    Finally, concentration should be controlled passively. Trying to concentrate harder doesn't improve concentration. Thinking about concentration or trying too hard to focus can even be distracting. Free up your mind and let things happen naturally. The only times when you must consciously focus is when you lose your concentration and need to regain focus. By using refocusing strategies explained later in this chapter, you can redirect your attention to task-relevant cues and block out harmful distractions.

    Is sum, concentration involves passively attending to task-relevant cues and blocking out distractions. Concentration is affected by confidence, physical intensity, and cognitive anxiety. Thus, you must find a way to maintain high confidence and control your emotions to maintain optimal concentration.

Summary Box 9.1

Concentration involves several elements:

1- Matching attentional focus to the demands of the skill
2- The ability to shift attention
3- Knowing what cues to focus on
4- Staying focused on those cues and blocking out distractions
5- Controlling arousal levels
6- The ability to refocus when distracted
7- Controlling your thought process

Concentration

Suggestions to improve concentration

1. Stay in the present

You must think about the shot that you have to make and not dwell on past events or think ahead. Thinking about the consequences of making or missing a shot will only divert your focus away from the actual shot. Be aware of when you lose your focus, and then refocus your attention on what you need to make a good shot. Take one shot at a time and challenge yourself to hit that one shot well.

2. Focus on performance cues

Find out what are the cues that you need to focus on to hit well and concentrate on those cues every time you swing. A lot of pros focus on their target because they know their body will react to the target. Having a target in your mind prevents other distracting thoughts from disrupting your concentration. If you are thinking about your target, you're not thinking about anything else.

3. Think about the process instead of the outcome

Outcome thinking is when you think about your score, what you'll shoot on that hole, or the consequences of your shot. They are irrelevant to the successful execution of your shot, thus you should not be thinking about them. Process thinking is when you focus on what it takes to hit well. It could be a swing key, your target, the ball, your rhythm, or your tempo.

4. Relax your mind and your muscles

When you are tense or anxious, you tend to become distracted. Attention narrows and you start thinking negatively or analyse too much. This may cause paralysis by analysis. The end result is that you are not focused on cues critical to performance.

5. Use self-talk

You can use trigger words to direct attention to what you must focus on to hit well. Use self-talk to encourage yourself and refocus. Positive self-talk can reduce anxiety and increase confidence, both of which will improve concentration.

6. Use imagery and simulation

Good simulation can go a long way to prevent choking. Simulate, through imagery or even concretely, situations where you might become distracted and think of what you can do to regain focus. Mentally rehearse every possible situation where you might lose your concentration, why this might happen, and how to regain focus. In addition, practice hitting golf shots with distractions. Have a friend try to distract you as you are hitting. This forces you to find strategies to block those distractions out of your mind.

7. Make a refocusing plan

This plan is derived from your imagery, simulations, and round evaluations. A refocusing plan includes all the physical and mental strategies to use when you lose focus. This plan might include a specific word, phrase, behavior, or thought that will get you back on track when things get out of hand (refer to Chapter 16 for more on refocusing plans).

8. Think positive

Positive expectations will improve your concentration simply because it increases confidence and composure. When you think negatively and are afraid of failure, your attention is not focused on task-relevant cues. Stay aggressive instead of playing defensively.

9. Develop a preshot routine

Developing a preshot routine will allow you to turn your concentration on and off during a round and ensure that you are mentally "fresh". You don't want to stress your mental resources when you are not playing.

A routine will also give you specific thoughts and behaviors to attend to and will prevent your mind from wandering aimlessly. A preshot routine will incorporate every strategy to enhance your concentration and will ready your mind as you prepare to hit a shot (refer to Chapter 12 for more info on preshot routines).

Summary Box 9.2

Strategies to improve concentration:

- ►   Stay in the present
- ►   Focus on performance cues
- ►   Think about process instead of outcome
- ►   Relax mind and body
- ►   Use self-talk
- ►   Use imagery and simulation
- ►   Make a refocusing plan
- ►   Think positive
- ►   Develop a preshot routine

Exercises to improve concentration & focus

Exercise 9.1: Centering

    Centering is the process through which you adjust your weight about your center of mass. Your center of mass is the point where vertical and horizontal lines separating your weight into two equal parts intersect (about 2 inches behind your navel). To center, close your eyes and take a deep breath from the abdomen (see Chapter 8 for specific instructions on deep breathing). Slowly exhale as you relax your neck, shoulder, and arm muscles. Think about the one point (center of mass) as you take your centering breath. The technique of centering will clear up your mind and adjust your anxiety level as well as muscle tension.

    Continue to take deep breaths and let your mind rest at the one point. Clear your mind of all thoughts. Let this happen naturally without trying to force it. If you can't clear your mind, don't wonder why or ask yourself questions. Quiet your analytical mind and continue to breathe deeply while focusing on the one point. Once centered, open your eyes and take in your surroundings. Be sensitive to what is around you without moving or turning your head. Enjoy the feeling of peace and serenity. Remain centered for a few more minutes. By the end of this exercise, you should feel relaxed and alert.

Exercise 9.2: Quiet Focus

Sit in a quiet room and imagine a red dot on the wall directly in front of you. Focus your attention on that small dot until everything else in the room becomes blurry. Keep your focus on the dot as long as you can without letting your attention drift away. Try changing the color and size of the dot while still keeping a tight focus on it.

Exercise 9.3: Golf Ball Fixation

Put a golf ball in front of you with the writings facing forward. Focus sharply on the ball. Notice all its fine detail and texture. Keep your focus on the ball for a minute or two, then focus on the writings on the ball. If you have distracting thoughts, gently bring your focus back on the ball.

Exercise 9.4: Switching Dimensions

Sit in front of your television and put a golf ball on top of it. Focus solely on the golf ball for about 1 minute. Then, turn on the TV. Try to keep your attention on the golf ball while trying to notice what is happening on the TV. Do this for about 1 minute. If available, turn on the radio on your stereo system. As you focus away from the ball, try to simultaneously take in information from both the radio and the television. Try to incorporate as much information as you can from both sources for about a minute. Now, turn your focus inward and try to remember all what you've seen and heard from both sources (1 minute). If this creates additional thoughts and ideas, let them flow freely through your mind. Then, shut out all other thoughts and focus on your heartbeat. Try to listen and count how many times your heart beats in a minute. Physically take your pulse if it helps you to focus on your heartbeat. Finally, focus sharply on the golf ball again. Try not to let anything disturb the connection between your mind and the ball. Remain focused on the golf ball for about 30 seconds.

Practice these exercises daily for about 5 minutes, and soon you'll notice improvement in your capacity to focus.

Distraction Control

Distractions are an integral part of golf and of life in general. Sources of distraction are nearly infinite, but can take on two forms: external and internal. External distractions are all the of the things in your environment that are not relevant to your performance, which is getting the ball to fly to its intended target. Examples of external distractions are:

▸ Course conditions
▸ Weather conditions
▸ Slow play
▸ Playing partners
▸ Spectators
▸ Loud noise
▸ Movement in peripheral vision

There are a large variety of external distractors during a round which have to be blocked out to prevent information overload. Whether something is a distraction also depends on each individual. What someone else views as a distraction may not be one for you. External events and stimuli become distractors only if you allow them to distract you.

Internal distractions can also make you lose your concentration. These distractors are the thoughts that are irrelevant to the good execution of the task at hand. Here are some examples of internal distractions:

▸ Past mistakes
▸ Worry
▸ Anger
▸ Overanalysing your swing

- fear of missing your shot
- negative self-talk and imagery
- expectations

One of the most common distraction golfers have are past mistakes. Dwelling on a bad shot often causes anger, frustration, or fear of failure. Another common distraction is thinking about your score or the consequences of making or missing a shot. These distractors take your focus away from what you need to attend to in your swing. Nervousness is also a recurrent distractor, especially in pressure situations. Again, things such as a pounding heart and shaky hands don't have to be distractors if you don't allow them to distract you. It isn't the shaky hands or the butterflies in your stomach that affect your shot, but the fact that you allow them to create negative thoughts diverting your attention away from what you need to do to get the job done.

In sum, it's your ability to block out any potential distractions and focus on performance-relevant cues that is important during a round of golf. However, it's important to know that fatigue can have detrimental effects on your ability to focus. More effort is needed to maintain focus when you're tired. The fatigue itself can become a distractor. If it's common for you to lose focus towards the end of a round, it may be because of fatigue. Good physical conditioning is therefore the best solution to improve concentration.

Exercise 9.5: Identify your potential distractions

Think of situations in which you get distracted in a round or at practice. What causes you to lose your focus in those situations? Were they internal or external distractions? Where was your focus when you got distracted? Use the above lists to help you. What were the circumstances leading up to your loss of focus?

Exercise 9.6: Identification of critical moments

Think about the critical moments where you tend to lose your focus. Is it on the first tee? After a string of pars? After the front nine? After a bad hole? Towards the end of the round? When do you need to remind yourself to concentrate? Identify these critical moments as precisely as possible and think about what you need to do during these moments. What has worked for you in the past? Write it down in the following space:

Here is a sample of a form that you can fill out based on the information gathered from the two previous exercises:

Table 9.1
Sample Distraction Control Chart

Critical Moment	Potential Distraction(s)	What to do
On the first tee	- People watching - Nervous about first shot	- Forget about the people watching - Have a good warm-up
After the front nine	- my score after 9 holes - muscles getting cold	- Don't count score - Stretch and stay warm
Birdie opportunity	- afraid to miss good opportunity - anxiety and pressure	- be aggressive — go for the hole - don't let physical symptoms of anxiety bother me

a blank copy of this chart can be found in Appendix A, p.219

Below are some exercises that will help you develop good distraction control skills. The goal of each of these exercises is to desensitize you to some potential distractors and incite you to develop strategies to stay focused.

Exercise 9.7: General Noise Training
Practice hitting shots in a noisy environment. Have a friend

talk or make noises while you're practising. If it's possible, practice somewhere where there is a lot of background noises. Are you able to block out the noises and concentrate on hitting the ball?

Exercise 9.8: Sudden Sound Training

Practice hitting shots in a silent environment but have someone make a sudden unwanted noise as you are taking the club back. It could be a cough, a shout (e.g., fore), a laugh, or any other noise that might break your concentration.

Exercise 9.9: Bad Weather Training

Practice in rainy, windy, or extremely hot conditions. Wet your hands to simulate rainy or hot conditions. When these conditions will be present during a round, they won't become distractions if you've learned to cope with them.

Exercise 9.10: Peripheral Movement Training

Practice hitting or putting with someone moving at the edge of your vision. Ask a friend to stand up, squat down, or move in any direction as you take the club back to hit your shot.

Exercise 9.11: Distraction Control Imagery

Think of a particular moment where you were distracted or use some of the distractions from Exercise 9.5. Visualize yourself in that distracting situation, seeing things through your own eyes. Try to remember every detail as vividly as possible. What was going through your mind as you were distracted? How did you feel at that instant? Now picture yourself blocking out that distraction as if it wasn't there. Go ahead and execute and perfect shot in your imagery.

Refocusing Strategies

More important than you ability to block out distractions is your ability to refocus after a distraction. Therefore, you need to learn and practice refocusing strategies to cope with inevitable distractions.

Concentration

1- Parking

Parking is a very useful technique to prevent you from dwelling on mistakes. When you "park" a mistake or a bad shot, you symbolically remove the distraction from your immediate consciousness to deal with more important information. To be effective, you must associate parking with a mental image that has personal meaning to you. For example, you can view bad shots, anger, or frustration as garbage. When you need to refocus, park these events/feelings away by "tossing out the garbage". Another example is to imagine storing mistakes in a file cabinet and closing the drawer.

It's also useful to have a physical trigger when you're parking errors. You might put your hand on a tree and "park" mistakes on the tree. The symbolic act often helps the process of refocusing after a bad shot.

2- Physical triggers

In addition to parking, physical triggers can also be used alone to refocus on the task at hand. Examples of physical triggers are: strapping the velcro on your glove, taking a deep breath, looking at the writings on the ball, tugging on your hat, pulling back your shirt sleeves, tapping the ground with your club.

3- Verbal cue words/ phrases

Cue words act as a verbal reminder to refocus when you are distracted. Examples of verbal cues are: "focus", "get a grip", "concentrate".

4- Mental image

You can also use a mental image that has personal meaning to you in order to refocus. Tossing out the garbage can be a good image. Slapping the little demon on your shoulder is another image you can use.

5- Sound/music

The use of a sound or a short song segment has been found to be effective to get your focus back on track. Again, choose something that has the desired effect on you.

All of these techniques can be combined in part or in whole to make the refocusing process more effective. The only rule is what works for you.

Exercise 9.12: Identification of refocusing cues

Think about some of the refocusing cues you've used successfully in the past as well as a few new verbal, visual, auditory, or physical cues that might help you refocus and write them down in a table similar to the one below.

Table 9.2
Sample Refocusing Chart

Refocusing Cue	Critical Moment
"get a grip"	anytime focus is lost
"just let it rip"	First tee shot
adjust shirt sleeve	before difficult shot
image of tossing garbage out	after a bad shot
"no guts no glory"	before a pressure putt

a blank copy of this chart can be found in Appendix A, p.221

The most important thing to remember about refocusing is that it should be practiced regularly. Follow this simple process to practice your refocusing skills:

1. Practice refocusing at home or in a calm and relaxed practice session to get used to different refocusing strategies.
2. Practice refocusing in more intense practice sessions, simulating pressure and game conditions.
3. Use your refocusing strategies during a round/competition.

Refocusing Exercises

Exercise 9.13: Bad Luck Training
You might hit good shots with poor results due to bad luck (e.g., poor lie, bad kick, gust of wind, tree limbs). Your ability to refocus instead of moaning and whining is essential as you walk up to the next shot. You can use imagery or go out and actually simulate bad situations. Give yourself bad lies (e.g., a divot, deep rough, uneven lies) or put yourself in any other difficult situations. Do this every 3 or 4 shots during practice.

Exercise 9.14: Sudden Sound Training B
This is similar to Exercise 9.8, except that you might ask your friend to intensify his distracting sounds so that it becomes nearly impossible for you to ignore it. Refocus while you step back and re-address the ball.

Exercise 9.15: Daily Hassle Training
Think of a bad experience or hassles you might have had during the day. Remind yourself of all the things you need to do or the bad shots you've made. Then, park all these negative things and refocus.

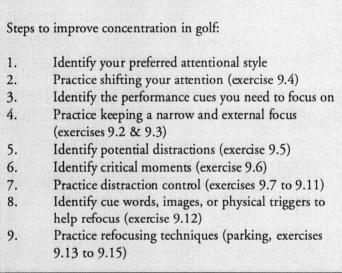

Instruction Box 9

Steps to improve concentration in golf:

1. Identify your preferred attentional style
2. Practice shifting your attention (exercise 9.4)
3. Identify the performance cues you need to focus on
4. Practice keeping a narrow and external focus (exercises 9.2 & 9.3)
5. Identify potential distractions (exercise 9.5)
6. Identify critical moments (exercise 9.6)
7. Practice distraction control (exercises 9.7 to 9.11)
8. Identify cue words, images, or physical triggers to help refocus (exercise 9.12)
9. Practice refocusing techniques (parking, exercises 9.13 to 9.15)

The Cantina

Welcome to the Cantina. If you've just completed the first nine holes, sit back and relax a bit. You deserve it. Hopefully, you've learned many things about yourself and how the mind affects your performances. You should now know what you should work on, and whether it's confidence, composure, or concentration, you have the basic mental tools to improve your weaknesses. If you've practiced the mental skills and applied the strategies shown so far, you should be well-prepared to face the back nine.

The last nine holes in this book is a more integrative approach to the mental skills you've learned on the front nine. If you've decided to start your reading here, get ready to jump right into the thick of things, for the following holes will give you many practical strategies to apply directly to your game. Don't hesitate to backtrack to previous chapters if you ever need further information on a subject.

Before you turn this page, take a moment to relax by doing some deep breathing. Let your mind go blank and focus on the one point. Do it now.

... Good. Now turn this page and start the last portion of this journey. Good reading!

Hole #10
Basic Principles

Par 5

Questions
Never: +2 Sometimes: +1 Always: 0

1- I always choose a clear target before each shot.
2- I have a positive focus when I'm playing.
3- I can stay in the present.
4- I trust my swing.
5- I accept the results.

Add 2 strokes to your score
Score:

Basic Principles

When you're on the course, it's important to think well if you want to get the most out of your game. If you've played the game for any substantial amount of time, you know that long hours of training and a good swing don't guarantee good rounds. By now you should know that your success on the golf course depends a lot on your state of mind. Why do you play well one day and poorly the next? Is it because you've lost your abilities overnight? Of course not. What are the factors that will help you play more consistently? If you've covered the first nine holes of this handbook, you know that Confidence, Concentration, and Composure are crucial to success. You've gotten information on how to improve those three crucial aspects of your mental game, but now you need to translate that knowledge into simple principles that you can remember and apply on a consistent basis on the golf course. To understand where these principles come from, we must first explore what peak performance is and what it involves.

Characteristics of Peak Performance

Have you ever played a few holes or maybe even a whole round of incredible golf where you get a surreal sense that everything is so easy? You have no worries or fears, and all you need to do is just take the club back and hit a great shot every time. If you've been in the "zone" before, then you know what I'm talking about. What you've experienced, in fact, is a period of peak performance.

Studies in peak performance or "flow" have revealed many common characteristics among athletes. A study done with competitive professional and collegiate golfers has revealed eight common categories characterizing peak performance:

- a narrow focus of attention
- effortless and automatic performance
- immersion in the present
- a sense of control over self and performance
- absence of fear or consequences
- high self-confidence
- a feeling of being mentally and physically relaxed
- experience of fun and enjoyment

Other researchers have also found these qualities in peak performances as well as a:

- positive and optimistic outlook
- time/space disorientation
- total immersion in the activity
- transcendence of self

It is important to emphasize that all of these studies state that peak performance is a temporary and sporadic phenomenon that is not under conscious control, but that can be induced more often by recreating the right mindset.

In sum, there seems to be a psychological profile associated with peak performance which involves the following characteristics: self-regulation of intensity, high self-confidence, high concentration, effortless control, positive thoughts and emotions, determination and commitment.

Thus, the key to entering the "zone" more often and for longer periods of time is to learn how to control and induce physiological and psychological states that will be more conducive to peak performance.

From these studies in peak performance, we can derive six basic principles that will help golfers establish a state of mind that will be more conducive to peak performance. These principles are the following: positive focus, present focus, precise target selection, commitment to the shot, trust in one's swing, and acceptance of the results.

Positive Focus

Anecdotal reports as well as research have proved that a positive focus is essential to achieving peak performance. Having a positive outlook builds confidence and helps manage emotions and concentration. A positive focus also prevents choking because you minimize the chances of falling into a negative performance spiral where negative thoughts lead to bad shots, and bad shots lead to further negative thoughts. By remembering good shots and forgetting about bad ones, you choose to dwell on positive events that maintain or increase confidence. You can use success imagery and see yourself executing a previous perfect shot in similar conditions. Positive self-talk is another effective tool to keep your thoughts positive. Not only will a positive focus help you play better, but you'll have a lot more fun playing.

Keeping focus in the present

Keeping focus in the present means that you must be focused on the task at hand and nothing else. You can't get ahead of yourself and think about the consequences of making or missing a shot. You need to focus on one shot at a time because in golf, every shot is important. Keeping a present focus also means not dwelling on mistakes or thinking about what score you can shoot. By doing this, you avoid distracting thoughts and emotions that can disrupt concentration.

Remember, the most important shot you have to make is always the shot you have to make right now. It's hard to stay in the present when you're about to achieve a very important goal, but you must catch yourself anytime this happens and refocus right away. Great players constantly monitor themselves because they know that it's a constant battle to stay focused on every shot.

Picking a precise target

Picking the smallest possible target sharpens focus and

enhances concentration. Having a target also allows you to focus on a task-relevant cue instead of negative and irrelevant cues. By focusing on a target, your brain tells your body where you want to hit the ball, not where you don't want to hit it. This will prevent you from focusing on things such as water and sand hazards, out-of-bound markers, or negative thoughts. Fixating on not hitting a ball somewhere only directs attention towards it. The nervous system knows no negation. Tell yourself "don't think of a golf ball". What is the first thing that came to your mind? Similarly, if you tell yourself "don't hit it in the water", you automatically gave instructions to your brain to focus on the water. The difference between winners and losers is that winners visualize what they want to happen, whereas losers visualize what they're afraid might happen. Thinking about your target tells your brain and your body where you want the ball to go.

In addition, having a target in one's mind will prevent other distractions from intruding one's consciousness and disrupt performance. The target "fills the void". Finally, by establishing a mind-target connection, the body will react to what the mind sees. Golfers that perform best are target focused, allowing nothing to disrupt the purity of their mind-body-target connection.

Committing to the shot

Once the target has been chosen, it is necessary to be fully committed to the club and type of shot one has selected. You can't let doubt or indecision cross your mind when you are about to hit because they cause distraction from task-relevant cues as well as a tentative swing. A strong commitment fosters positive expectations. Positive expectations, in turn, will produce better results than negative expectations.

Trusting one's swing

Trusting your swing means that you give up conscious control and let things happen at an unconscious level. Don't burden your mind with swing mechanics because conscious thoughts often hinder a repetitive and rapid skill such as the golf swing. A well-learned automatic skill such as the golf swing will be impaired when too much conscious control is exerted. There's only one place for swing mechanics, and that's at practice. On the course, you must learn to trust what you have trained and let it happen.

Accepting the Results

We are humans, and that means we sometimes make mistakes. You can't expect to hit perfect shots all the time. You must accept the results and move on to the next shot. You can't dwell over a great shot or a bad shot because in golf, every shot is important. Dwelling on negative events distracts the mind from task-relevant cues and may cause paralysis by analysis because when things don't go well, we tend to analyze or think too much and stop trusting our swing. You have to understand that perfectionism will cause more harm than good on a golf course. Golf is perhaps the only sport where we lose more than we win. Thus, learning to accept adversity and defeat is essential to keep a positive focus. Not only will it make you play better, but your whole experience will be more pleasant. Accept your shots regardless of outcome. If the results are positive, use them to boost your confidence. If they're negative, tell yourself that this only gives you more chance of making the next shot. Take it as a challenge to hit the next one well.

As you can see, the main principles behind good golfing are simple yet hard to apply. Most people know these principles, but applying them consistently and at the right time is the challenge that every golfer faces. Once you succeed in applying these principles consistently, you'll get a lot more enjoyment out of the game and you'll score a lot better too.

Instruction Box 10

- ▶ Keep a positive focus
- ▶ Stay in the present
- ▶ Pick a precise target
- ▶ Commit to the shot
- ▶ Trust your swing
- ▶ Accept the results

Hole #11
Anchoring

Par 3

Questions
Never: +2 Sometimes: +1 Always: 0

1- I can vividly relive past experiences.
2- I can control my emotional state effortlessly.
3- I can quickly call up desired feelings when I want.

Add 1 stroke to your score
Score:

Anchoring

The process of anchoring is a powerful technique that will help you to instantaneously call up feelings, thoughts, and behaviors. Anchoring derives its power from principles in classical conditioning. Remember Pavlov's dog? If you've learned about it in high school or college, you know what I'm talking about. To put it simply, if you ring a bell every time you feed the dog, the bell will become associated with food. After a certain period of conditioning, ringing the bell alone can make the dog salivate in anticipation for food. It happens because subconsciously, the dog has formed an association between the bell ring and the arrival of food. The bell, in this case, became an anchor.

Although the human mind is a bit more complex than a dog's, there are many examples that illustrate how unconscious anchors guide our behavior. For example, students do better in exams when they are in the same room in which learning occurred because part of their environment has become anchored to learning and a focused state. Music is another powerful stimulus that becomes anchored to a certain emotional state. Ever noticed how people associate different songs to situations, feelings, or experiences? That's because something happened or was happening when they heard the song. The song, in this case, became an anchor. When you repeat a story amongst friends, you relive the same feelings that you had when you were there the first time. Finally, irrational fears and phobias are salient examples of associations that have been formed at a certain point and have endured because of their strong emotional link. People have physical and emotional reactions to objects, odors, and sounds that may not provoke any particular experience in someone else. Why? Because an association has been formed in the past. Sometimes it will take a few occurrences, sometimes the emotional experience is so strong that it takes just one instance to form an indelible association for life. These associations are so powerful that often they are hard to break. It is a mechanism instilled by evolution in all of us because it has a strong survival value. This innate ability, if harnessed, becomes a powerful tool to control your mind and body.

An anchor is set when a stimulus (visual, auditory, kinesthetic, olfactory, or gustatory) is present at the peak of an intense experience. In other words, if a stimulus is consistently applied at the peak of an intense state, it will become neurologically associated with that state. Once the association is formed, the anchor can trigger the same state regardless of external circumstances.

The implications of all of this is that you can create anchors that will trigger a desired state or behavior at any time, regardless of what is going on inside and outside of your mind. For example, you can create anchors to trigger feelings of confidence, calmness, intensity, focus, aggressiveness, or any other state you desire. If your anchor has been well established, then it will trigger the desired state when you "fire it".

Creating an anchor

1- Recall or induce a state

Use imagery to recall a past experience as vividly as possible. Relive every moment through you own eyes, experiencing it as if you were there again. See, hear, feel every detail as vividly as possible. While you're reliving the experience, it's very important that you see it, feel it, or hear it by being "inside" your body (see imagery chapter for more on internal perspectives). The more intense the state, the stronger the anchor will be.

2- Introduce a specific stimulus

When you feel that you're near the peak of the experience,

introduce a specific word, image, sound, or behavior. The second important factor besides intensity, is timing. The application of an anchor can last up to 15 seconds. Kinesthetic anchors will typically run longer than other types of anchors. Application of the anchor will stop at the peak of the experience. It is applied just before the peak, and ends when you peak.

The uniqueness of the stimulus is also an important factor to consider, because if it is something that is continually present, then the anchor will loose its power because the association will weaken with time and random exposure. If an anchor is continually triggered randomly, then it won't be linked to a desired state. If you use a kinesthetic anchor on a part of your body, then it should be a part that is seldom touched (an ear instead of a finger).

3- Charge your anchor

To charge an anchor up, you usually need repetition. The anchor has to be associated with the internal state or experience repetitively to be consolidated (unless you use a spontaneous anchor that has been automatically linked to a very intense emotional state). This means that you need to introduce your anchor in association with the desired state numerous times to give it power. You can do it through imagery by reliving a desired state (a time where you were confident, calm, and focused for example), and introducing your cue at about 75% of its peak and keep it there until you reach the peak point of the state. If the anchor and the target state are continuously repeated together with the right timing, they will become associated together.

You can also stack different experiences into a single anchor to charge it up. For example, you can charge up your anchor by using a moment where you hit a great shot off the tee, another where you sank a very long putt, or when you won a tournament and were walking towards the 18th green triumphantly. You can even use non golf-related experiences to conjure up a state of absolute confidence and self-control. Charging your anchor can happen through imagery and in actual moments where you feel that you've reached a desired state. If you're on the golf course and hit a great shot and feel good about it, there's no reason why you shouldn't anchor it. The more experiences which bring about a similar state (e.g., confidence) you stack into an anchor, the more powerful the anchor becomes.

4- Put your anchor in context

Once an anchor has been well-established, you can choose to transfer its power to another anchor that is more in context to situations where you think this anchor would be useful to fire. For example, if you've anchored a state of confidence by squeezing you ear lobe, it might be a little strange to do it on the course. Thus, you can choose an anchor that could more easily fit into your preshot routine. Let's say you wanted to use the sound of strapping the velcro on your golf glove. To transfer your anchor, just fire your established anchor, then as soon as you experience the desired state, strap the velcro on your glove. You can also repeat the same process by which you first created the original anchor as well, but this time by using the new anchor. After a few repetitions, your new anchor will have the same power as the original one.

5- Reinforce your anchor

You need to maintain your anchor regularly so that it doesn't loose its potency. If you don't periodically reinforce your anchor, its power will diminish and eventually fade away. The association between the desired state and the anchor need to be repeated every now and then for the anchor to last.

Finally, not all anchors are equally powerful. Visual people will respond better to visual anchors (images, colors, etc), auditory people will respond better to words or sounds, and kinesthetic people will respond better to touch and movement. In addition, the uniqueness of the anchor is important in regards to its power.

Summary Box 11.1

Anchors are dependent on:

- ▸   Intensity of desired state
- ▸   Timing
- ▸   Repetition
- ▸   Uniqueness of linked stimulus
- ▸   Context in which the association was formed

Exercise 11.1

1.   Choose a desired state that you would like to reproduce (e.g., confidence, concentration, calmness and serenity). Identify a specific time when you felt like that and re-experience it through vivid imagery. The more detail you put in your imagery, the more salient the emotion will become. See through your eyes the details of objects and people, hear the sounds and words associated with the experience, and feel the sensations in your body. Try to be aware of the behaviors and thought patterns associated with your desired state.

2.   Select a unique anchor to associate with that desired state. Relive the desired state again as vividly as you can, and when you feel you're about to reach the intensity peak of the state, begin anchoring your chosen cue. For example, if you chose to squeeze the skin between your fingers (kinesthetic anchor), you would start squeezing it when you feel the intensity at about two-thirds of its peak, squeezing harder as the intensity rises. When you think you've reached the peak of the state, release the pressure and stop the anchoring process.

3.   Repeat the second step several times and charge your anchor

more each time by making the desired state more vivid. Enhance the vividness of the desired state by amplifying color, brightness, volume, sharpness, etc.) and involve all five senses.

4.   Clear your mind and fire your anchor to test its power. You should be able to recall the desired state spontaneously without much conscious effort if you've effectively charged up your anchor. Repeat step 3 and 4 as often as required until you can call up your desired state effortlessly.

In sum, anchoring is a powerful tool for calling up confidence, concentration, relaxation, creativity, learning, and other resourceful states. An anchor can direct focus of consciousness to important experiences and help you consolidate knowledge and transfer learning and experience to all kinds of situations.

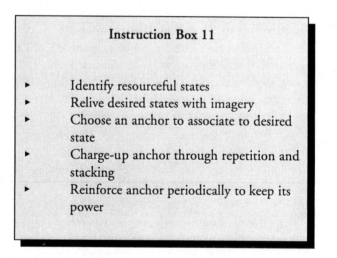

Instruction Box 11

► Identify resourceful states
► Relive desired states with imagery
► Choose an anchor to associate to desired state
► Charge-up anchor through repetition and stacking
► Reinforce anchor periodically to keep its power

Hole #12
Performance Routines

Par 4

Questions
Never: +2 Sometimes: +1 Always: 0

1- I use a clear and structured preshot routine.
2- I follow my routines even when things are not going well.
3- I use a post-shot routine.
4- I have a routine between holes.

Add 2 strokes to your score
Score:

Performance Routines

The development of individualized performance routines combines all of the basic skills and strategies learned thus far and incorporates them into concrete, practical, and context-specific actions. All of the previous training in stress management, confidence building, imagery, self-talk, and concentration is put together into performance routines that will help you regulate your thoughts and emotions before and after each shot. Each component of the routine is developed and refined in a personal way and integrates all the strategies needed to achieve an ideal state of mind to play the golf of your dreams.

The Preshot Routine

Most shots are determined in the moments just before you hit the ball. Therefore, it is important that you be fully concentrated before each shot. Because so little time is spent on actually executing a shot in comparison to the overall length of a round, it's hard to concentrate continuously for more than four hours. Thus, we must find a way to switch our concentration on and off if we want to remain mentally fresh (and have fun).

A preshot routine involves a consistent and set patterns of thoughts and behaviors that you execute before each shot. It's main purpose is to ensure that you are mentally and physically ready before each shot. On the physical side, the routine will take care of your grip, stance, posture, and alignment. On the mental side, it will get you into your ideal state of mind. In other words, a consistent routine will make sure you are confident, decisive, and focused each time you step up to the ball.

The length and content of a routine depends on your personal preferences. Experiment with different lengths of time to see what feels most comfortable. If you are someone who likes to play quickly, then use a short routine. If you are someone who likes to be thorough, perhaps a more complex routine is required. There is no standard or ideal preshot routine. The best routine is one that feels natural and instinctive to you. The most important thing in a routine isn't so much the content, but just the fact that you have one that is consistent and repetitive.

The preshot routine is effective because it helps direct attention towards task-relevant cues while keeping your thoughts consistent, thus prevents you from being distracted by external events or worry and fear. However, it takes time and practice to develop a sound preshot routine. You must continually refine your routine until you feel comfortable with it and feel it is helping performance. The more you practice it, the more it becomes ingrained in your mind, and the more it is effective. Hence, it is essential to incorporate your routine into your practice. This will also allow you to transfer your practice more easily to the course. A consistent preshot routine becomes a habit that you consistently rely on in any situation, especially under high pressure. Often, golfers will stop using their routines when things don't go well, but it is precisely during those moments that you need to stick to your routine if you want to bounce back.

Finally, your routine will most likely be different for full shots, chips, and putts since the demands for each type of shot are different. Chipping and putting require more emphasis on feel and fine-touch, whereas full shots are more about power and accuracy. Your routine, thus, will reflect those differences in terms of content.

What can a preshot routine consist of?

A trigger

Some players like to start their routine with a gesture that reminds them that their preshot routine has begun and it's time to focus on it. It may be just putting a hand on top of a club, strapping the velcro on your glove, or a tugging at your shirt sleeves.

Performance Routines

A cleansing breath

You can use a one-breath relaxation procedure to calm yourself down and rid yourself of any anxiety or physical tension.

Neck-shoulder scan

Every time you step up to the ball, you can do a quick scan of areas that are often tense. In most cases, the neck and shoulder area is where tension can disrupt a golf swing. Other areas to scan are forearms and grip tension. Do a quick scan and relax any muscles that might be tense (see Chapter 8 for more on relaxation).

Selection of a target

Once you make a decisive choice about the club and what type of shot is needed, you must pick a small and precise target. You can do this standing behind or next to the ball, whichever you prefer. I might also be helpful to pick an intermediate target anywhere from 2 to 5 feet in front of you. The shorter the shot, the closer the intermediate target will be to you.

Some form of imagery

This is perhaps the most personal element in a preshot routine. Imagery can be visual, auditory, or kinesthetic (see Chapter 6 for more on imagery). Some people easily see their shots, others hear them better, and yet others prefer to feel their shots. If you can do all three simultaneously, your imagery can be more vivid and effective. Some players find it helpful to visualize the ball's trajectory in the air, where it will land, roll, and stop. This often instills confidence in a golfer and makes him feel that his vision somehow programs his body to execute the kind of shot desired. A lot of people also like to replay their best shots in that particular situation in their mind. Again, this can inject a healthy dose of confidence in you.

Practice swing(s)

Once your mind is calm, focused and you are confident about your shot, you might want to take some practice swings. Practice swings can be used to improve feel and confidence. You can use practice swings with imagery to program your brain and your body for the right execution of the desired swing.

You can take practice swings behind or parallel to the ball, with or without imagery. This is a matter of personal preference. Some players visualize their shot, then take a practice swing. Others might take a swing while visualizing. The most important thing about a practice swing is that it should make you feel comfortable, confident and decisive about your shot. Try to keep the number of practice shots constant, but be flexible about it as well. If the last swing didn't feel right, you shouldn't hit when doubt and indecision threaten to destroy your shot. It's better to take a couple of more practice shots to make sure you're confident and decisive.

Another important things to do during your practice swing is to be focused on the target instead of burdening your mind with swing mechanics. If you really must think about mechanics, do it in your first practice swing(s), because you should solely be concentrated on target and feel during the last practice swing.

Waggles

Waggling the club is an effective strategy to relax and loosen your muscles. Try to keep the number of waggles constant, but be flexible. Remember that the purpose of the waggle is simply to make you feel comfortable just before you take the club back.

The Swing

The final step in the routine is perhaps the most important. Look at the target, look at the ball, and swing. Don't stand over the ball too long once you take that last look at the target. You must allow your mind-body-target connection to remain pure because any further delay is an opportunity for unwanted thoughts to distract your mind and interfere with your unconscious reaction. This doesn't necessarily mean you must rush your back-swing. Practice your routine often enough so that you develop a pace that fits your personality. The simpler the routine, the easier it'll be to follow. And if for any reason, you still don't feel ready to make your shot after going through your routine, don't be afraid to back up and restart it from the beginning.

Finally, you must not be so dependant of your preshot routine that if for any reason you are unable to use it completely, you hit a bad shot. Make sure you have a backup plan to quickly get into a good frame of mind when you cannot execute your routine. Be consistent, but don't be obsessive.

It may take some time and fine-tuning to develop your ideal preshot routine. It will also take discipline and commitment to adhere to it no matter what the circumstances, but the end result is more consistency and, consequently, more enjoyment.

Sample Preshot Routine

- ▸ Adjust cap to start routine
- ▸ Take a deep breath and relax
- ▸ Stand behind ball and pick target
- ▸ Align body and club with intermediate target
- ▸ Take one practice swing to loosen muscles
- ▸ Step up to the ball, take a deep breath, look at target and visualize the ball landing there
- ▸ Look down on the ball, feel the perfect shot
- ▸ Look at target, take a deep breath, waggle twice, look back at the ball, and swing

---

Post-shot Routine

Because there is a tendency for golfers to focus on negative thoughts after a shot, post-performance routines are needed to switch from a negative mode of thinking to a more positive and effective mode of thinking. A large part of a post-shot routine is about emotional control. A post-shot routine serves to keep your composure and concentration regardless of results. It is designed to help you accept your shot, forget about it, and stay positive.

The first part of a post-shot routine can involve a release of emotion. It's good to let out a little bit of steam after a bad shot. After all, we are human and such reactions are unavoidable. You can avoid frustration and anger from building up by allowing yourself to release your emotions with a simple word without feeling guilty about it. This doesn't mean that you can spend your time swearing on the golf course or throwing your clubs around. Release your frustration in a controlled manner, then move on.

Next, you can use a rehearsal swing from the place where the bad swing occurred. Do a perfect swing to show yourself that you can actually do it the next time. This will prevent you from keeping negative image in your mind and replace it with a positive image.

Another step in the routine is to forget about the last shot because no one plays perfect golf. The shot belongs to the past, and dwelling on it will do you no good. A technique such as parking can help you to forget about a bad shot.

Finally, the last step in a post-shot routine is to refocus. You need to regain your concentration by calming yourself down with self-talk, relaxation or any other strategy that you use to regain focus. This allows you to approach the next shot with good concentration and confidence. This is where you should use your verbal, visual, auditory, or physical anchors to refocus.

Between-play Routine

A round of golf takes many hours to complete and is punctuated by long periods of inactivity. Therefore, effective strategies are needed to keep thoughts positive and concentration optimal. As a routine between each hole, you can rehearse good shots from the previous hole to keep confidence high and thoughts positive. In addition, it's important to temporarily switch concentration off as you walk to the ball in order to stay mentally fresh. Some of the things you can do are the following: imagine personal relaxing experiences, talk with your playing partners, admire the scenery, whistle or hum a little song. The important thing is to do something that is enjoyable and takes your mind off golf for a little while. Doing this prevents you from dwelling on mistakes or engage in negative thinking.

Instruction Box 12

▸ Elaborate performance routines
▸ Practice routines
▸ Refine routines

Hole #13
Self-Monitoring

Par 4

Questions
Never: +2 Sometimes: +1 Always: 0

1- I evaluate my game after a round.
2- I assess what I did well and what I didn't do well after a round.
3- I evaluate why I played well or poorly.
4- I draw lessons from my round or competition.

Add 2 strokes to your score
Score:

Self-Monitoring

It's important to constantly monitor and evaluate yourself in order to refine your mental strategies. If you can learn from each round, good or bad, you will improve much more quickly. After a round, sit down and think about what you did well, why you did well, and what you can do to improve next time. If you know what makes you play well and what makes you play not so well, you will be able to use this information to your advantage in future rounds.

Draw some lessons from your round, especially bad ones. Bad performances are great learning experiences. Take personal responsibility for your performance and tell yourself that you can only improve if you learn from it. Ask yourself these questions:

What was responsible for my performance?
When did I started hitting well/badly?
What was I thinking about?
How did I feel?
What was I focused on?

Knowing yourself is the first step to getting the most out of your performance. It will allow you to target what needs work instead of just going out to the range and hit hundreds of balls. Fix the problems, then go home and forget about them. The next time you play, you'll know what to do to achieve your best performance.

You can use forms such as the one on the next page to help you evaluate your game (also included in Appendix A, p.223).

Self-Monitoring

Name: Date:

Personal Stats

Total Score:	Front:	Back:
Fairways:	Greens:	# Putts:
Eagles:	Birdies:	Pars:
Bogeys:	Double Bogeys:	Other:

These questions are designed to help you reflect upon your game and to help you develop or refine your routines and game plans.

1. Did you have a performance outcome goal for this event?

2. If so, to what degree did you achieve this performance outcome goal?

Did not achieve   0 1 2 3 4 5 6 7 8 9 10   Achieved goal
goal at all   completely

3. What was your on-site goal(s) for this round (e.g., what focus did you want to carry into this round?

4. To what degree did you achieve this on-site focus goal(s)

Did not achieve   0 1 2 3 4 5 6 7 8 9 10   Achieved goal
goal at all   completely

5. Circle your feeling *going into this round.*

No determination   0 1 2 3 4 5 6 7 8 9 10   Completely determined

No anxiety   0 1 2 3 4 5 6 7 8 9 10   Very anxious

No physical   0 1 2 3 4 5 6 7 8 9 10   Highly activated
activation (flat)   and pumped up

6. Rate your level of Confidence in this round:

No confidence   0 1 2 3 4 5 6 7 8 9 10   Completely confident

Self-Monitoring

What was the main reason(s) responsible for this confidence level?

7. Rate your level of Concentration in this round:

   No concentration   0   1   2   3   4   5   6   7   8   9   10   Completely concentrated

   What was the main reason(s) responsible for this concentration level?

8. Rate your level of Composure in this round:

   No composure   0   1   2   3   4   5   6   7   8   9   10   Very composed

   What was the main reason(s) responsible for this composure level?

10. How did your preparation go?

   Terrible/ no preparation plan   0   1   2   3   4   5   6   7   8   9   10   Really well

   Were you feeling the way you wanted to feel?

11. What were your thoughts as you approached this round?

12. How did your game plan go?

   Poorly/ no game plan   0   1   2   3   4   5   6   7   8   9   10   Really well

   What elements of the plan went well, what did not, what needs work or adjustment?

13. What were you focused on when at your best during this round?

14. What were your thoughts before each successful shot?

15. What were your thoughts before each bad shot?

16. Were you distracted at any time during the round?

If yes, what was the cause(s) for this distraction?

17. Did you have to refocus at any time during this round?

If yes, what did you specifically do to refocus?

Did the refocusing strategy work immediately?

18. Review this evaluation form. What lessons can be drawn from this round?

Psychological Scorecard

You can use a psychological scorecard to help you monitor your mental game. Each time you play, let someone else hold the normal scorecard. That way, you won't be too focused on outcome and you'll put less pressure on yourself to shoot a certain score.

The scoring system shown below will help you assess what elements of your mental game are going well and which require further attention. It will help in your self-evaluation and goal-setting. The scorecard can also give you feedback while you play so that you can make adjustments that will have an immediate and positive impact on your attitude. A perfect score on the scorecard would be 110 (prep=2; PF=18; Routine= 18; Concentration= 54; Reaction= 18).

A. Preparation

Before teeing off on the first hole, give yourself a score from 0 to 2 for preparation. This is your subjective view of the quality of your preparation for the round (see Chapter 15 for more on preparation). An optimal preparation would earn a score of 2, and minimal or no preparation would be 0, 1 being an adequate preparation. Here are some quick pointers for a good preparation:

- stretching
- hitting a few full shots
- hitting a few chips & putts
- strategic plan of first few holes
- use of any mental strategy to optimize mindset

Remember, preparation is personal, so the content and duration will depend on your personal preferences. Find out what kind of preparation works best for you, and rate yourself according to those criteria. (Max = 2)

1. Positive Focus (PF)

Positive focusing is a method of directing your attention to the better aspects of your game. After each hole, record all good or better shots, mentally replay those shots before the next tee off, and forget about the bad shots.

Recording good or better shots

These are shots that are better than average shots. Don't be too hard on yourself in judging your shots. Rate the quality of the shot, not the results. If you hit a good shot but got a bad bounce, record the shot on your scorecard. Use abbreviations to record each good shot on each hole. Here is a short list of abbreviations you can use:

Woods: D = driver; 2W-9W = 2-wood to 9-wood
Irons: I1-I9 = 1-iron to 9-iron
Wedges: PW= pitching wedge; SW = sand wedge; LW = lob wedge
Chips: 6C-PWC = 6-iron chip to pitching wedge chip
Bunker shots: club used + B; SWB = sand wedge in bunker
Putts: LP = long putt (10 feet or longer); P = 5 to 9-foot putt; SP = short putt (4 feet or less)

Replay good or better shots

While walking towards the next hole or while waiting on the tee, take a few seconds to mentally replay the good shots that you recorded on your scorecard. See, hear, and feel those good shots through your mind's eye. Recreate the experience, how you were feeling just prior to hitting the shot and what was going through your mind. You can recall things such as grip pressure, flight of the ball, feel of good ball contact, etc. This should only take a few seconds once you get use to doing it, so don't worry about slowing down play. If you don't have time, try to review at least one successful shot. By doing this, you are forced to think about your good shots instead of the bad ones.

For each hole, give yourself a checkmark if you recorded and replayed at least one good or better shot. (Max = 18)

2. Routine

For each hole, give yourself a checkmark if you followed your preshot routine on every shot. For example, if you selected a target, committed to the shot selected, and went through the rest of your preshot routine, give yourself a checkmark. Remember that a routine will include both physical (posture, grip, alignment, stance) and mental behaviors (imagery, relaxation, self-talk). (Max = 18)

3. Concentration

After each hole, give yourself a score from 1 to 3 on concentration. For example, if you were concentrated on every shot, give yourself a 3. If you only lacked concentration on 1 shot on a par

4, give yourself a 2. If you lacked concentration for 50% of your shots or more, give yourself a 1. (Max = 54)

4. Reaction

On each hole, give yourself a checkmark if you reacted positively to every shot. That means using only positive verbal statements when describing your game or yourself, defending against negative comments (from yourself and from others), keeping your attributions positive (causes you assign to outcomes or events), forgetting and refocusing for the next shot. An example of a post-shot routine can be found in chapter 12. If you did all of the above things for each shot, give yourself a checkmark. (Max = 18)

After each round, count your mental score and set some goals to increase it with each subsequent round. Things might seem complicated at first, but you'll see that after using the psychological scorecard for a few rounds, scoring yourself will be relatively simple. To help you assimilate this method, start focusing on just 2 of the 4 aspects (e.g., positive focus and routine). As it becomes easier to score yourself, add the 2 remaining aspects (concentration and reaction).

Instruction Box 13

- Keep a psychological scorecard
- Fill out evaluation form at the end of each round
- Use lessons learned from forms and scorecard to refine preparation, practice, and mental plans

---

Hole #14
Practice

Par 5

Questions
Never: +2 Sometimes: +1 Always: 0

1- I have a clear plan when I practice.
2- I have a clear goal for practice.
3- I hit as well on the course than at practice.
4- I spend at least 60% of my time working on my short game.
5- I pick a target and go through my preshot routine even in practice.

Add 2 strokes to your score
Score:

Practice

There can be two categories of golfers at the driving range. Those who just mindlessly hit ball after ball, and those who have a clear goal, pick a target and go through their routine on every shot. A lot of recreational golfers, especially high handicappers, would fall into the first category. Most of the time, golfers don't get anything out of practice because they don't practice playing golf, but hitting balls. If you're just hitting one ball after the other, you're just exercising.

How often do you hear people say: "If only I played as well as I practice"? Often, these golfers hit great shots in practice because they swing freely, without any fear of failure or mechanical thoughts to burden their mind. On the course, however, they have to aim their shot, and all of a sudden they think about all kinds of things instead of being focused on making the shot. You can't transfer your practice game to the course if you don't practice in a playing state of mind.

What does a quality practice involve?

Have a clear goal

First, you need to have a clear goal of what you want to achieve. Top Olympic athletes in all sports always have a clear practice goal. The same holds true for top touring professionals. They know what they want to accomplish before each training session, and they set goals and make a commitment to achieve these goals.

Practice like you play

This means that every shot in practice means something. You

have to put yourself in the same frame of mind as when you're on the course, which means that every shot you make is important. Therefore, you need to be fully concentrated on each shot, pick your target, and go through your preshot routine because that's what you do on the course. In addition, change targets and clubs often because you'll seldom get two consecutive similar shots on the golf course. It's easier to hit a good shot when it's the 10th you've hit with that club. By practicing this way, you simulate game conditions that will help you transfer your practice to the course.

Improve problem areas

Most people like to practice their good shots but neglect to work on their weaknesses. If you want to improve, you need to work on shots you have trouble with. Leave your ego at home if you want to become a better golfer.

Practice shot-making

For good players, it's sometimes hard to know the difference between effective and ineffective practice. It's easy to become wrapped in our own ego because we're hitting the ball beautifully. You might think you're the greatest golfer in the world since you can hit great shots almost every time you swing the club. You just hit great shot after great shot, admiring them as if you were pausing for a magazine. People look at you in amazement, wishing they would be able to do the same thing only half the time. However, on the next day, on the course, you hit a beautiful 7-iron that soars high in the air, but the strong winds suddenly grab the ball and pull it left of the hole, and the ball falls short and in the deep left bunker. You make bogey, and wonder why you couldn't score better even though you hit "perfect" shots. What you should've done the day before was practice the kind of shots that you needed to make when you're playing. This means that you need to practice shot-making. If you know that the conditions will be windy, practice keeping the ball low. If you are playing on a course with a lot of pins requiring a fade on the approach, then practice fading the ball. If there's a lot of sand, practice sand shots. You have to prepare yourself for your round. You must remember that the purpose of practice isn't to win a hitting contest, but to get you ready to play a round of golf.

Practice with a performance mindset

The performance mindset involves trusting your swing, going through your routine and putting yourself in a playing state of mind. The same basic principles that apply on the golf course also apply in practice (see Chapter 10 for basic principles). Training in this mindset will help you transfer your practice game to the golf course. Practice like you play, and you'll play like you practiced.

Thus, training in the performance mindset is essential before a round, especially competition. To trust your swing on the course, you need to spend time doing it at practice. In pressure situations, your dominant habit will always take over. If you're used to analyze your swing and think negatively, this will happen every time you're under pressure. Most golfers spend the bulk of their time analyzing their swing, and they carry this dominant habit on the course, where they should instead trust what they have trained and let things happen unconsciously.

However, it's important to point out that practice can be purely mechanical. It's good to get away from the playing state of mind when you're working on your swing. You might need to hit ball after ball without going into your routine when you're working on something mechanical. It depends on your practice goal. When you practice like that, you practice with a training mindset. The training mindset is essential when you want to work on swing fundamentals or swing changes. In most cases, beginners are more likely to train with this mindset.

You might want to spend more time in the training mindset at the beginning of the season, when you're trying to restore the proper mechanics after a winter layoff. As the season progresses and your swing is grooved, you'll need to spend more time in the performance mindset. As a general rule, spend about 60% to 70% of your time in the training mindset and 30% to 40% in the performance mindset early in the season, and reverse the percentages as you progress through about the midway point of the season. Just before a round or competition, almost all of your practice time must be spent with a performance mindset.

Practice your short game

More than half of your shots on the golf course are within a hundred yards of the hole. Yet, most people spend the bulk of their time hitting drivers. However, the quickest way to lower your handicap is to improve your short game. Review one of your rounds. How many strokes did you make from a hundred yards or less? If you could shave off one missed approach here, one bad chip there, and a couple of short putts elsewhere, what would you have shot?

When it comes to shots that don't require a full swing, feel is very important. And the only way to develop feel is by practicing extensively. Big drives feed egos, but the short game lower scores.

Recreate pressure situations

Pressure is another factor that is found on the course but not at practice, so somehow you need to find a way to recreate it. You can use imagery and simulations to recreate game pressure, then practice strategies to keep your composure and concentration (see Chapters 8 and 9).

Practice your mental game

Every mental skills and strategies need to be practiced at the driving range if you want them to be effective on the golf course. Go through your swing keys, focusing cues, relaxation strategies, distraction control and refocusing strategies, and practice your preshot routine. You can't expect imagery to be effective on the golf course if you've never done it in practice. Similarly, a routine doesn't become routine unless you practice it.

Have fun

Having purposeful practice doesn't mean that it has to be boring. You can do a lot of things to put a little fun into it. You can simulate a round, imagining the holes in your mind and hitting with the appropriate club based on your previous shot. You can create all kinds of little games that, while being fun, get you to focus and concentrate on each shot as if you were on the course. Use your imagination to make practice more fun and effective. And remember, quality should always be emphasized over quantity. Trying harder, practicing longer, or analyzing in greater detail don't usually result in lower scores. It usually just takes away the fun.

Summary Box 14.1

Recommendations for quality practice:

- ▸ Have a clear goal
- ▸ Practice like you play
- ▸ Improve problem areas
- ▸ Practice shot-making
- ▸ Practice with a performance mindset
- ▸ Improve your short game
- ▸ Recreate pressure situations
- ▸ Practice your mental game
- ▸ Have fun

Suggestions to make practice more fun

- ▸ *Round simulation*: You can imagine a 430-yards Par Four with water on the right and sand near the landing zone on the left. Pick a target that would be a spot on the fairway where you want the ball to land, and hit your shot. If you made a 250 yard drive where you aimed, hit a 5-iron next. If you hit it left, imagine yourself in the rough or in the sand and play the appropriate shot. You can simulate an entire round like this.

- ▸ *Closest to the flag contest*: If you're there with a friend, you can have friendly competitions such as who can get the ball closest to the flag. This little game can be used for irons, chips, or sand shots. Have a friendly wager. Most people bet during a round, so might as well do it in practice. This forces you to concentrate on your shot because there is something at stake.

▸ *Putt out contest:* Start with a putt three feet from the hole. Each time you make the putt, back up two feet for your next putt. If you miss, move forward a foot. The winner is the first one to reach the fringe or the furthest from the hole after a set time.

▸ *Chipping contest:* This game works well if you're more than two. The first person makes a chip, and if the next person chips closer to the hole, the previous one is eliminated. If, however, the next chip is not closer to the hole, than the previous person picks up his/her ball and goes back in line. The ball that is the reference is always the one from the previous person. If someone holes a chip, the previous person is obviously eliminated, and the next person's chip serves as the new reference. The game goes on until there is only one survivor left.

Instruction Box 14

- Practice with a clear goal
- Always pick a target
- Change targets often
- Switch clubs frequently
- Use your preshot routine
- Improve your weaknesses
- Practice shot-making
- Practice with a performance mindset
- Practice your short game
- Recreate pressure situations
- Simulate game situations
- Rehearse mental strategies
- Use games to make practice more fun

Hole #15
Preparation

Par 4

Questions
Never: +2 Sometimes: +1 Always: 0

1- I come to the course early to stretch and warm-up.
2- I play well right from the beginning of a round.
3- I follow a consistent warm-up routine before a round.
4- I make a plan of what to do once I get on the course.

Add 2 strokes to your score
Score:

Preparation

How many times did you see a professional golfer arrive 5 minutes before his/her tee time, rush to the first tee, do a couple of warm-up swings, and then start playing? Yet, a lot of amateurs and recreational golfers do this. It is no wonder that they have inconsistent performances. Top touring pros make a structured plan before each tournament regarding course management and shot-making strategies. They also plan their time and know when to wake up, how long to stretch and warm-up, when to eat, when to get to the course, how long they'll practice, and when to arrive at the first tee.

While this might seem too much for the average recreational golfer, there is no reason why you shouldn't have a preparation plan that you can execute before each round. Preparation is personal, so find out what works best for you. You may already have a preparation routine, but ask yourself how it can be improved. Use all the information gathered from the first chapter on self-awareness as well as all subsequent chapters to know what you need to get into an optimal frame of mind. Can you make a plan to make sure that you feel the way you want to every time you play golf?

Consistent performances start with consistent preparation. If you want to be ready to play your best, you need to be adequately prepared to do so because peak performances rarely occur if your preparation is left to chance. Hence, good preparation ensures that you are physically and mentally ready to play golf and promotes peak performance as well as preventing injuries.

Exercise 15.1

What kind of preparation has worked well for you so far?

Preparation

Write down the physical and psychological warm-up that has been most helpful. What did you specifically do?

Exercise 15.2

Make a list of things you want to do before your round. Also write down your desired thoughts and feelings as well as the images, triggers or cue words that you will use to achieve them. You can use a form such as the one found below.

Table 15.1
Sample Preparation Chart

Physical Activity	Psychological Activity	Strategy
Stretch	Visualize first few holes	find quiet place
Hit a few drives	Adjust intensity level (ZOF)	deep breathing and centering
chip and putt	Maintain confident attitude	positive self-talk

a blank copy of this chart can be found in Appendix A, p.227

Pre-Competition Plans

Once you find out what kind of preparation works best for you, it's time to put it into a pre-competition plan. The reason why you should develop pre-competition plans is to have a consistent approach before each competition or round. This plan will tell you what to do physically and mentally to perform at your best level.

Although many of the steps that will be outlined in the following paragraphs are intended to be used by serious golfers at a competitive level, recreational golfers can benefit from this detailed approach to golf as well.

1. One week before competition

Your pre-competition plan should start a few days to a week before the actual competition (although it can start for weeks before if it's a major competition). Here are some of the items that you should consider in your plan:

- ▸ Acquire information about the competition site
- ▸ Check details regarding travel and accommodation
- ▸ Check and pack equipment
- ▸ Check and pack any other relevant personal belongings (e.g., this book)

Once you've taken cared of those details, you should do a day-by-day plan on how you will get ready for your first round. For example, what and when to practice and for how long? Typically, you'll take care of any problem areas in your swing as early as you can, then start fine-tuning your game as you approach the competition to stay sharp. Don't forget to practice with a performance mindset, especially during the last two or three days before competition. Most players will have intensive practice sessions until two days before their first round. You want to allow yourself a full day of rest or very light practice to allow your body to recover. If you practice too much before a competition, you might be burned out when competition begins. This is especially important for recreational golfers, who tend to hit a bucket or two the day before their round. Thus, it's important to plan your practice sessions leading to a round or competition. Most players will fine-tune their mental approach the day before competition while allowing their body to rest. You can also use positive self-talk and success imagery to build confidence.

Summary Box 15.1

Preparation: 1 week before competition

- Fix problems as early as possible
- Fine-tune your game to stay sharp
- Allow a full day of rest to recover
- Build confidence through positive self-talk and success imagery
- Practice with a performance mindset
- Review mental game plans

---

2. Night before competition

The night before a competition is often used to review course management and to optimise your mental game. Many professional golfers will play the course hole-by-hole through imagery. This helps build confidence as well as reinforce tactical strategies. You might also want to do some deep muscle relaxation or any other relaxing activity. Repeat positive and empowering statements to increase confidence and stay positive. Finally, make sure you get appropriate sleep.

Summary Box 15.2

Preparation: Night before competition

- Review course management strategies
- Make sure equipment is ready
- Relax
- Use positive self-talk & imagery
- Simulate round
- Get appropriate sleep

---

3. Competition morning

Allow plenty of time to eat and get ready to go to the competition site. Wake-up early enough to avoid rushing. Be careful not to eat too much to avoid feeling sluggish. Also allow enough time to digest your meal before playing. You don't want to be too hungry or too full during your round. For example, a meal consisting of fresh fruits, muffins, and cereals 90 minutes before a round would be appropriate. As you wake up, have a list of positive statements to read in order to feel good right away.

When you get to the competition site, familiarise yourself with the installations (bathroom, locker, restaurant, driving range, putting green, chipping area). Arrive early enough to avoid rushing. Most pros will get to the golf course at least an hour before their tee-off time. When you rush, you get disorganized, don't have time to warm-up properly, feel anxious, and are not totally concentrated and ready to play. Use more positive self-talk and imagery to rehearse success.

Summary Box 15.3

Preparation: Competition morning

- ▸ Don't rush
- ▸ Eat light
- ▸ Think positive -- self-talk & imagery
- ▸ Get familiar with installations

---

4. Warm-up

The warm-up is not a time to improve your swing or try new shots. It's used to see what kind of swing you brought to the golf course and how your swing feels. You should be focused on feel, tempo, and rhythm instead of mechanics. This part of your pre-competition plan should be extremely consistent and well rehearsed. This is the moment you get into your personal "bubble". Do a final review of the course and how you plan to play each hole and use all the mental strategies to get you into an optimal mindset.

Guidelines for a good warm-up

Stretch well

Have a stretching routine to execute before swinging. After a few stretching exercises, use long, slow swings with a weighted club to loosen the muscles involved in a swing. A good stretching routine will not only get your body ready to play but will prevent short-term as well as long-term injuries.

Focus on balance and tempo

Take a few swings to hone balance and tempo, especially if you tend to have a quick tempo early in the round or are a little stressed. Find a comfortable tempo before you play.

Don't think about mechanics

Professional players try to avoid overloading their mind with mechanics before a round. You want to start trusting your swing and let go of conscious control. If you can't swing with an empty mind, find a swing thought that works for you that day, and try to stick to it.

Check your alignment

During your warm-up, you want to pick a target to see if your alignment is good. Every shot on the course will be target-oriented, so it's very important to be properly aligned.

Start with short clubs

You want to start with shorter clubs because they put less strain on your body than longer clubs. Save long irons and woods until your muscles are loose.

Don't hit too many shots

Don't hit too many shots because you don't want to be too tired at the end of your round. Most pros like to hit around 35 to 45 full shots during their warm-up.

Sharpen you short game

Hit a mixture of chips, lobs, and sand shots before playing because you can be sure to have a few of these to hit during your round. Chipping and putting is the best exercise to get into a playing state of mind.

Get a feel for speed

Most pros like rolling long putts to gauge green speed. Roll some long putts to the fringe to focus on speed. Finish by holing short putts to build confidence.

Do intensity and anxiety checks

You don't want to be too physically charged or nervous before you play, nor do you want to be too flat. Check intensity/anxiety levels at different points during your preparation phase and, if necessary, adjust it with the proper techniques learned previously.

Think positive

Have a list of positive self-statements to repeat and use some success imagery to develop a positive frame of mind before performing.

Arrive early on the first tee

Arrive with time to spare on the first tee to take care of last minute chores (scorecard, playing order, club count, balls & tees, etc.). Also, it will allow you time to assess weather conditions and visualize your first shot.

Summary Box 15.4

Guidelines for a good warm-up:

- Stretch well
- Focus on balance and tempo
- Don't think about mechanics
- Check your alignment
- Start with short clubs
- Don't hit too many shots
- Sharpen your short game
- Get a feel for speed
- Do intensity and anxiety checks
- Think positive
- Arrive early on the first tee

Table 15.2
Sample Pre-Competition Plan

Timeline	Physical Preparation	Psychological Preparation
Night before	- Prepare golf bag & lunch - Review plan for tomorrow - Plan for 8 hours of sleep	- Relax by listening to calm music - Review course management strategies - Successfully play course with imagery
Morning 3h before tee-time	- Shower and breakfast - Light exercise & stretch	- Positive self-talk to establish optimistic outlook - Relax and review plans

Before leaving for the course	- Check if everything needed in car	- Listen to relaxing or energizing tape in car, depending on intensity level
At golf course	- Go to marshalling area to report in	- Don't rush — relax - Soak up the atmosphere and conditions
1h before tee-time	- Stretch for 5 minutes, ending with long and slow swings with weighted club	- Deep breathing - Positive self-talk
Warm-up: 50 minutes	- Start with a few easy pitching wedges (5-10 shots) - hit about 5 shots each for 9, 7, 5, and 3 iron, respectively - Spend about 5 minutes hitting drives - Check alignment	- Evaluate weather conditions - Positive thinking – "I will play well", "I am ready" - Check intensity level and muscle tension - Ideal focus – evaluate most appropriate swing key
	- Spend about 15 minutes hitting chips, lobs and bunker shots - Spend about 10 minutes putting, rolling long putts first to gauge speed and finish by holing short putts	- Evaluate course condition - Positive self-talk: "I'm sharp today", "Today's your day" - Relax muscles — deep breathing - Review focus cues - Sharpen feel

5-10 minutes before tee-time	- Check golf bag -- clubs, balls, tees, water. - Get scorecard	- Last intensity/anxiety check - Positive imagery - Plan first hole - Review game plan in light of weather and course conditions

a blank copy of this chart can be found in Appendix A, p.229

You might also want to develop an alternate plan in case for any reason, you can't carry out your plan. List what you want to do and how you would like to react if things don't go well (waking-up late, bad weather, heavy traffic). If you had to abbreviate your preparation, what are the most important things you need to do?

Table 15.3
Sample Alternate Warm-Up Plan

Physical Preparation	Psychological Preparation
- Sign in - Check equipment	- Keep thoughts positive - Deep breathing
If enough time: - Roll a few putts to gauge green speed - Hit a few chips	- intensity/anxiety check - Use focus cues to keep mind focused on relevant cues
- Go to 1st tee - Stretch - Take a few warm-up swings	- Review strategy for first hole - Take deep breaths while stretching - Positive self-talk – "no problem", "I'm ready", "Go for it"

Remember that you shouldn't hit any shots, putt, or chip without going through your entire preshot routine. Rushing to hit a few balls won't do you any good if you do not take the time to mentally and physically prepare for each shot. It's always useful and time-saving to use your mental strategies while you are stretching or warming-up when time is a factor.

In addition, you may need two pre-competition plans, one for days when the warm-up is going well, and one for days when the warm-up is not going so well. Finally, it's important to evaluate and review your plans regularly.

Good planning and preparation will ensure that you are loose, alert, and focused before playing and will ensure the best possible start. This is where all of the strategies and skills learned in the previous chapters are brought together so that you have a detailed protocol to optimal preparation.

Remember, if you fail to prepare, you prepare to fail.

Instruction Box 15

- ▶ List all activities leading up to competition
- ▶ List preferred preparation activities
- ▶ List strategies to achieve optimal mindset
- ▶ Build pre-competition plan(s)
- ▶ Act on plan
- ▶ Review plan and adjust as needed

Hole #16
Mental Plans

Par 4

Questions
Never: +2 Sometimes: +1 Always: 0

1- I make a game plan on how to play each hole.
2- I make a plan defining how I need to focus during a round.
3- I make a refocus plan to cope with distractions.
4- I follow my mental plans even when things don't go well.

Add 2 strokes to your score
Score:

Mental Plans

After learning how to increase your confidence, concentration, and composure through skills such as self-talk, imagery, and relaxation, it's time to put it all together into personal working mental plans. The previous chapter has already discussed one of these plans in regards to preparation (pre-competition plan). This chapter will teach you how to make tactical plans as well as competition focus and refocus plans.

The Tactical Plan

Professional players always go into a tournament knowing how to play each and every hole. They make a tactical plan about what strategies to use for each shot. Amateurs, however, rarely plan ahead. They just take the driver out of the bag whenever they can and try to hit the ball as far as they can. You see people getting into trouble all the time because they failed to plan on how to play each hole. The purpose on a mental plan is to let you adopt strategies that will give you the best chance of scoring well by playing on your strengths and minimizing any weakness in your game.

First, examine the course you'll be playing and plan how you would like to play each hole. Make a plan regarding landing zones, target and club selection, and hazards to be avoided. Every pro does this, and so should you. If you've never played a course before, then you'll need to improvise, but you can always look at the distances and diagrams on the scorecard, and ask playing partners about how each hole should be played if they've played there before. Make up a plan at each tee. It's better than no plan at all.

Mental Plans

The best way to plan for a hole is to mentally walk backwards, from the green to the tee. Looking at the hole this way can reveal much more information about the best landing areas and forces you to think about what clubs to hit, and where you want each shot to land.

Having a good tactical plan avoids any unnecessary risks and will put you in a better position to score well. You don't need to use your driver if you can't reach a tight par 5 in two. It's sometimes better to hit a 3-wood or an iron off the tee for better accuracy. Play to your strengths. If you're not comfortable with approaches under 100 yards, then leave yourself a full pitching wedge instead by selecting the appropriate club on your previous shot. There's no use on hitting a driver 60 yards from the pin when you can hit a safer 3-wood or 2-iron 100 yards from the pin. Be aggressive, but adopt a conservative strategy. Always play for wide areas of the fairway and be realistic when you're in trouble. Instead of going for the green by trying to squeeze the ball through branches and get yourself into more trouble, pitch it out on the fairway to have a clear approach. Play smart.

Finally, your game plan should also include different scenarios for changing course and weather conditions. You might play a hole differently under wet/dry conditions or under calm/windy conditions. Maybe you'll approach certain holes differently depending on how you are playing. If you feel extremely confident and decide to go for it, always weight the risk and benefits.

Summary Box 16.1

Tips to consider in a tactical plan:

- ▸ Always plan the best course of action for each hole
- ▸ Mentally review the hole backward when planning on how to play it
- ▸ Play to your strengths
- ▸ Stay aggressive but adopt a conservative strategy
- ▸ Play for wide areas of the fairway first
- ▸ Don't take unnecessary risks when in trouble
- ▸ Include alternate strategies for changing game conditions

---

The Focus Plan

The purpose of the focus plan is to give you a structured approach to carry your focus through the whole round or competition. It's kind of like a recipe that tells you what to do to adhere to the 6 basic principles outlined in Chapter 10. Some people don't like the idea of approaching the game in such a structured fashion, but the focus plan can really be nothing more than just a few key phrases that will allow you to get into the right frame of mind during important moments in your round. You don't have to lose your spontaneity or be mentally rigid to make a plan, but you don't want to leave your performance to chance neither. After all, that's what mental training is about. Just like anything else, the contents of the focus plan will depend on your needs and preferences.

The first step in designing a focus plan is to identify critical situations during a round of golf. These act as checkpoints to ensure you are still playing at an optimal level, mentally and physically. For example, some of the critical situations in golf can be: the first tee, after the front nine, after a string of birdies or pars, after a couple of double-bogeys. At these critical moments or checkpoints, you can scan your body for muscle tension, check anxiety levels, redirect attention on relevant cues with self-talk, and use confidence building strategies. The goal is to stay in your desired mindset throughout the whole round.

Exercise 16.1: Critical situations

What are your critical moments? Write down any situation that you feel is important and critical to your performance in a round of golf. It can be when you're on top of the leader board, when there are people watching, when you're behind by a couple of strokes, towards the end of the round when you feel tired, or any other situation you find is important for you to remind yourself to stay focused.

Exercise 16.2: Critical Cues

Now that you've identified some of those critical situations, it's time to define what needs to be done during those critical moments.

Should you include a body scan for muscle tension? What are the anchors (image, expression, or physical trigger) that will help you deal effectively with those situations? What do you want to think about or say to yourself?

Table 16.1
Sample of critical situation chart

Critical Situation	What to do
At the first tee	Say to yourself: "you're ready for a great round", take a deep breath, ignore the people that might be watching and concentrate on your routine. Think tempo and rhythm.
After a bad hole	"forget about that hole", park it on the green, do some positive focusing
In the lead	Don't look at leader board, stay aggressive, concentrate on tempo and feel
Towards the end of the round	Breathe deeply, drink a lot, enjoy the scenery between each shot, don't think about fatigue or score, "strong finish", "ain't over 'till that last one drops", manifest emotions after each good shot to pump up.

a blank copy of this chart can be found in Appendix A, p.231

It might also be useful to have a general cue that you can use to maintain your focus and stick to your game plan throughout the round. Expressions such as: "smooth and easy", "don't sweat it", "stick to the plan", have been found to be effective for many golfers. Go back to previous chapters on self-talk, composure, imagery, concentration, and confidence to refresh your memory about what you can do to get yourself into an ideal state of mind.

In sum, think about how you want to feel, focus, and function during the various parts of a round. Then, work out a plan (it can be chronologically sequential, i.e., from Hole #1 to Hole #18) to make it happen. Use the information gleaned from Hole #1 as well as from your evaluation forms and psychological scorecard (Chapter 13). Remember to continually rehearse and refine your plan as you learn more about yourself.

The Refocusing Plan

The refocusing or distraction control plan allows to cope with distractions and unexpected events. Chapter 9 has already covered some ground on distraction control and refocusing strategies. However, things will sometimes not go as smoothly as you plan. You must therefore be flexible enough to cope with potential problems and changes.

The refocusing plan covers "what if" scenarios before and during a round of golf. It allows you to make the best out of less than ideal conditions. Things such as being late, bad weather and course conditions, a bad warm-up, unexpected delays, personal problems or crises, and equipment problems can steer you off course and prevent you from playing to your potential if you don't know how to deal with them. A great round or putt from another competitor could be a distractor as well as a missed putt. You need to tell yourself that every putt you miss increases the odds of making the next putt. You must learn to deal constructively with problems whenever they occur. Don't let an occasional slice, missed putt, or poor approach distract you for the next two holes.

For golfers who enter into multiple-round competitions, sources of distraction can be very high and overwhelming. The most important thing for them is to know how to deal with these distractions and stay focused on what they need to do to perform at their best. The best golfers on the PGA, SPGA, and LPGA know that it's best to control only what is under their immediate control. Paying attention to uncontrollable factors/events is just a waste of time and energy.

Exercise 16.3: "What if" List

Make a list of all the possible problems or distractions that you can encounter from the morning before a round to the end of the round. Consider how you would like to cope with each of these scenarios. Example of such scenarios are: bad weather, bad course conditions, getting caught in traffic and not having your usual warm-up time, running out of tees or balls, losing a club, slippery grip, losing some spikes, delay in start time, old injury acting up, negative comments from someone, bad news, a bad warm-up, poor putting, bad drives, slow partners, etc.

Summary Box 16.3

Building a refocus plan:

- ▸   Identify potential distractions (exercise 9.5)
- ▸   Make a contingency list (exercise 16.3)
- ▸   Identify strategies to use for each contingency or distraction
- ▸   Rehearse refocus plan
- ▸   Refine refocus plan

Finally, it's extremely important that you remind yourself not to think too much. Having mental plans can sometimes make golfers think too much. When this happens, your attention is turned inwards and is no longer on cues critical to performance (see Chapter 9 for more on attention and concentration). You might experience paralysis by analysis if you constantly think about what you should do and say to yourself. That's why it's important that the mental plans be well rehearsed and practiced so that you don't have to constantly think about them on the course. When you're playing, you just want to have fun and let things happen. Your mind and body already know what they're supposed to do if they're well-trained.

Instruction Box 16

- ▸ Build a game plan for each golf course
- ▸ Use information from exercise 1.2 & 1.3 in Chapter 1 and evaluation forms in Chapter 13 to build a competition focus plan (exercises 16.1 & 16.2).
- ▸ Build a refocus plan
- ▸ Rehearse mental plans
- ▸ Stick to your mental plans
- ▸ Refine mental plans

Hole #17
Putting

Par 4

Questions
Never: +2 Sometimes: +1 Always: 0

1- I love to putt under pressure.
2- I can feel the right distance for each putt.
3- I aim for the hole.
4- I believe I can sink long putts.

Add 2 strokes to your score
Score:

Putting

The putter is the most used and important club in your bag. Good putting is more important than anything if you want to score well and win tournaments. On a physical level, putting is a fairly simple task. Just roll the ball in the hole. On the mental side, however, putting can become your worst nightmare. Therefore, knowing how to use your mind to putt better can be more useful and less expensive than a new putter, putting lessons, or a new teaching aid.

The secret to good putting is a golfer's attitude and how he approaches each putt. You must love putting and relish every opportunity of making a pressure putt. That's how every good putter thinks. A positive attitude is the first step to improve your putting. Once you have a positive attitude about putting, you must believe that you are or can be a good putter. Confidence is essential to any shot in golf, but especially putting. Every time you step up to the ball, you must believe that you can sink the putt.

Another important skill in putting is to develop a good feel for speed. Feel is not only important for speed, but also for the line you select on a breaking putt (the amount of break in a putt depends on its pace). A strong sense of touch or feel can avoid a lot of three-putts and give you more confidence.

Phil Mickelson, when asked about what made him such a good putter, replied that he simply concentrated on making a good stroke and good contact every time he putted. Thus, you need to focus on the execution of the putt, not on the outcome. You don't have to sink every putt to call it a good putt. Concentrate on reading the green, choosing the appropriate line, aiming correctly, and trusting your instincts.

In Chapter 6, the importance of imagery was explained. Good imagery skills are essential in your ability to see the line, how the putt will break, and how fast the ball will roll. If you can imagine these things distinctly every time you putt, your chances of making it will be much higher.

Summary Box 17.1

Important skills to putt your best:

- ▸ Positive attitude about putting
- ▸ Belief and confidence in yourself
- ▸ Good feel
- ▸ Focus on execution, not on outcome
- ▸ Good imagery skills on the green
- ▸ Trusting your stroke

Suggestions to improve putting

▸ Get a good read on the green. If you are a competitive golfer, use your practice rounds to find out as much as you can about each green. Make notes that you can carry with you during your round. If you're just a recreational golfer, observe other player's putts and chips to help you see the breaks better. Reading greens is an art that comes from experience and good imagination.

▸ Aim for the hole: It's obvious that you should aim for the hole when putting, yet many people just want to get it "somewhere around the hole" on long putts. It makes a huge difference when you go for it on every putt. You give yourself a much higher probability of success when you want to sink your putt, no matter how far away. Going for the hole gives you the greatest margin of error because even if you miss, you're still "somewhere around the hole". Your focus is also sharper than if you just aimed at a general area. With sharper focus, comes better concentration.

- Visualize your line: Putting becomes much easier if you are able to see how the ball will break and how fast it will roll. Even golfers who play by feel "see" their line distinctly. You need to have a good idea of the path the ball will take once it leaves your putter head. For many golfers, this sort of clear vision happens sporadically and spontaneously, but you can make it a habit with practice. If it has happened to you before, you know how helpful it can be. Try to see the ball roll on its intended path and fall into the cup every time you putt.

- Develop a good feel for speed: Again, feel is very important for assessing how much speed you need to put into your stroke. Practice rolling some long putts to develop a strong sense of touch. Do it with your eyes closed sometimes to get better kinesthetic awareness.

- Use self-talk: Encourage yourself each time you face a difficult putt. Self-talk can help you direct your focus on execution and stay confident (see Chapter 5 for more on self-talk).

- Focus on feel and tempo during your practice strokes: Practice strokes serve to ingrain the right feel and should ultimately be exactly what the real stroke will be like. This is when you can match the stroke you see and feel in your mind with a real stroke. A practice stroke is no time to be focused on mechanics.

- Aim with your eyes over the line: Aiming correctly is critical to the success of a putt. You might have the right line, but if you don't aim on that line, you won't roll the ball where you're suppose to. It's helpful to have an intermediate target in the same line to help with alignment. Align your putter head with that target, then align your body around the putter head.

▸ See the target with the third eye: Nick Price continues to see the target in his mind's eye even when he is looking at the ball. We can't look at the target during a stroke, but that doesn't mean we can't continue to "see" it. Having an image or a clear feel for where your target is will make the body react to it. We are wired so that our body will respond to what we see.

▸ Don't hesitate: When you're ready to putt, do it. Don't second-guess your line or your speed. Go through your putting routine, then let go. The more time you spend over the ball, the more opportunity you allow for doubt, indecision, and worry to invade your mind and ruin your execution.

▸ Accept the results: Just like any other shot, you must accept the results and move on. Dwelling on a missed putt will only bring you closer towards failure. Learn from your putt, park it, and refocus on what you need to do in the here-and-now. Not being able to accept the results is the first step towards the "yips".

Summary Box 17.2

Suggestions to improve putting:

- ▶ Get a good read
- ▶ Aim for the hole
- ▶ Visualize your line
- ▶ Develop a good feel for speed
- ▶ Use self-talk to keep confidence and focus
- ▶ Focus on feel and tempo during practice strokes
- ▶ Aim with your eyes over the line
- ▶ Continue "seeing" the target with your third eye
- ▶ Don't hesitate
- ▶ Accept the results

The "Yips"

Many golfers have an imaginary disease called the "yips". The yips is an uncontrollable fear of missing a putt that destroys your putting ability. It starts with a few missed putts, which creates a fear of missing, which results in more missed putts, which results in more fear, tension, and doubt, which ultimately creates an irrational fear of putting. These golfers then turn to technical changes and buy all kinds of training aids without much success. Thus, they label themselves as having the yips, a hopeless disease that prevents them from putting normally like everyone else. However, the truth is that there's no such thing as the yips. It only exists in a golfer's mind. Viewing your putting skills as a disease (yips) is just an excuse for not accepting the consequences of your behavior.

The first step in curing the yips is to face the irrational fear of missing a putt. Fear, worry, and doubt create tension in your muscles and disrupts your already tentative putting stroke. The desire to steer the putt as well as excess tension can do all kinds of bad things to your putt. You can push it, pull it, leave it short, or just jab at it and watch it roll 5 feet past the hole. You can't control your muscles and have a smooth stroke if you're too anxious. Intense anxiety also causes you to loose feel, a very important factor in putting. Finally, when you step up to the ball hoping not to miss a putt or leave it too long or too short, you are certainly not focused on making a smooth stroke and good contact, and you're certainly not confident about making the putt. As research has demonstrated, confidence is an essential factor contributing to the success of putting.

Suggestions for beating the yips

- Don't think about the consequences of making or missing a putt. Thinking about the possible result only creates unwanted anxiety and fear. Stay in the present and focus on making a good stroke and good contact.
- Forget about the past. You can't take back all the putts you've missed, so might as well forget about them. In doesn't matter how well you putted before, it's how well you putt now that counts. The present putt is the first putt of the rest of your golfing career.
- Avoid labelling a putt as a "must-make" putt. Every putt counts for one stroke, whether you're 20 feet or 1 foot from the hole. Feeling that you must make a certain putt only creates a fear of missing. A putt is a putt, and all putts can be made.
- Awaken the child within. Have you ever seen a kid with the yips? Kids putt well because they only have one thing in mind: to put the ball in the hole. They don't think about consequences or about technique. They just do it.

Summary Box 17.3

Suggestions to overcome the yips:

- Don't think about consequences and outcome
- Forget about the past
- Don't label your putts
- Putt like a kid

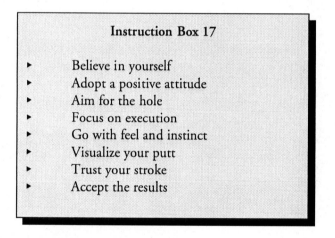

Instruction Box 17

- Believe in yourself
- Adopt a positive attitude
- Aim for the hole
- Focus on execution
- Go with feel and instinct
- Visualize your putt
- Trust your stroke
- Accept the results

Hole #18
Specific Problems

Par 4

Give yourself a bogey if more than 11 questions apply to you
Give yourself par if between 6 and 11 questions apply to you.
Give yourself a birdie if less than 6 questions apply to you.

Score:

Q: I don't have fun on the course anymore? What can I do?

A: If you're not having fun, chances are you're taking golf too seriously. It's easy to get wrapped up in our own ambitions. You must remember the reason why you played golf in the first place. Perhaps you are thinking too much about outcome. Focus on the process instead of playing for score (see Chapter 3). Also, be wary of perfectionism, because it will push you towards negative thinking and takes away the fun. Finally, maybe you are thinking too much on the course. Next time you play, just go out there and have fun. Don't think about anything else than just the pleasure of playing golf in a beautiful setting.

Q: No matter what I do, I can't seem to improve. Is this as good as I'm going to get?

A: Perhaps it is as good as you will get. But that's unlikely. You'd be surprised at how much you can accomplish. We are only limited by our own visions. All golfers go through a certain period of stagnation. The key is not in working harder, but smarter. In fact, working harder and longer can make things even worse. Remember that it's the little things that make a difference. Take things more lightly, and focus on enjoyment. Sometimes it's even good to take a little time off so that you can come back fresh. Do some performance profiling (Chapter 1). Direct your energy on your weaknesses. Furthermore, work on your short game and putting. That's the first place to look if you want to improve on score. Perhaps the mental training in this handbook will help you take your game to the next level.

Q: I play well on only one nine. Why is this?

A: There can be various reasons why you play poorly after a great front nine. Your beliefs about your abilities may be one of the reasons. How you label yourself as a golfer often affects how you perform. Here's why. If you think you are a bogey player, for example, you will think you are playing over your head after a great front nine. When this happens, you start feeling extra pressure to keep that hot streak going. You don't want to squander a potential good score and start playing defensively. Your swing gets tentative and your muscles tense up. As soon as you make a few bad shots, you get frustrated because you're saying to yourself that you're blowing up this great opportunity to shoot a low score. With each hole, pressure builds up inside and that's when people often start to over-analyse. By this time, your muscles are really tense, your mind is distracted from the task at hand, and your swing becomes mechanical and unnatural. Everything is effortful. In sport psychology, we call this "paralysis by analysis". All of this happens because you're thinking about consequence and outcome instead of staying in the present and play one shot at a time.

When you start down this road, you forget every basic mental principle that a golfer should apply when on the course. You are not focused on your shot, distrust your swing, and have difficulty accepting the results. Needless to say, this is a recipe for disaster.

On the other hand, here's what happens in the case of a bad front nine followed by a good back nine. Because you played poorly on the first few holes, you're probably saying to yourself that you've already messed up your round and have nothing to lose anymore. You adopt a carefree attitude and swing freely, without thinking about consequence or outcome. You don't over-analyse your swing and just let things happen. All of a sudden, you realize that you're playing well and are on the way of saving your round. Unfortunately, you final score always remains in the same range, and this reinforces your belief about what kind of player you are.

A bad front nine is often the result of poor preparation or poor focus on the first couple of holes. Some players hit bad shots because they are so nervous on the first tee. They lose confidence after a bad start and it takes them a while to get back on track. Good preparation and a sound preshot routine may help you start your round on the right foot.

To break out of this circle of stagnation, you must first change your limiting self-beliefs (see Chapter 4). It's always preferable to label yourself as a better player than you really are. That way, when you're in a hot streak, you don't think that you're playing over your head.

This removes pressure because it's normal for you to play this well. Use imagery to imagine yourself playing a consistent round of golf. Picture yourself making birdies and pars. You must restructure your thinking to convince yourself that shooting a certain score is well within your reach.

Second, commit yourself to play one shot at a time and forget about the consequences of missing or making that shot. Stay in the present and focus on your target. Because we are not perfect, this isn't always easy to do. However, each time you get ahead of yourself, use it as a trigger to renew your commitment to routine. Having a good preshot routine to resort to in times of pressure is a great way to play more consistently (see Chapter 12).

Third, use positive self-talk to calm yourself down or help you focus on your shot. Many top athletes constantly talk to themselves, either silently or loudly. What you say to yourself must be encouraging and supportive. You know yourself best, so you know what can bring out the desired reaction (see Chapter 5).

Fourth, make a refocus plan (see Chapter 16). Your plan should include the actions and strategies you want to use should your concentration falter. It's useful to imagine yourself in a situation where you start hitting a few bad shots after playing well on the front nine and decide on how you would like to handle the situation. Simulate in your mind every type of situation and see yourself reacting in an ideal way. This will help you to take the right actions and refocus should things actually go wrong on the course.

Finally, adopt a carefree attitude. Enjoy the opportunity to play golf in a beautiful scenery while others may be trapped in a small office at work. Don't put so much importance on your score. Put things into perspective. You're out there to have fun, so enjoy yourself.

Q: I'm playing better, thinking better, but my scores haven't gone down. Why?

A: You must remember that when you reach a certain level, scores go down much less rapidly. For example, getting from 85 to 75 happens in a constant progression, but going from 75 to par is a much more lengthy process. It might just take more time than usual. In addition, target what can make you score better. Do the performance profiling found in Chapter 1. Work on your putting and your short game. You can always improve on those. Finally, check your self-beliefs (Chapter 4). Are your beliefs and attributions limiting your performance?

Q: I don't want to think or plan too much out there. I just want to have fun. How can I combine mental training into that philosophy?

A: The whole purpose of mental training is to make performance more automatic, so there's no problem combining the two. Work on your mental game at home and at practice. On the course, just let go. It might be a little hard in the beginning because you have to have a certain awareness to improve, but with practice, application of mental skills will become second-nature.

Q: Why do I always seem to play better with a new set of clubs for a while, then go back to normal?

A: Again, this might be because of self-beliefs (Chapter 4). When you have new clubs, you are expecting to be a better player, so you play better. After a while, the novelty effect wears off, and you're back to normal. You can either imagine yourself having success with old clubs, or always think you're playing with new clubs that will give you a performance edge. At any rate, changing your beliefs is much less expensive than buying a new set of clubs or a new putter every now and then.

Q: Why do I always have trouble with particular holes?

A: The reason why you have trouble with certain holes may be related to your strengths and weaknesses. A particular hole may not be suited to your game. When this is the case, a good plan on how to play the hole is necessary (Chapter 16). Think about your strengths and weaknesses (Chapter 1) as well as the challenges the hole presents you with. Another possible reason is that bad experiences on that hole resulted from poor course management, and this negative result has been anchored in your mind. Thus, every time you play that hole, the negative memories and beliefs affect your performance (see Chapter 4).

Q: I always seem to play poorly with certain partners. Why is that?

A: This is probably a problem in concentration (Chapter 9). When you play with certain people, you might try to impress them, or be impressed by them. When this happens, your thinking changes and the way you approach each shot changes as well. You might not be focused on the performance cues that generally help you hit good shots. In addition, you tend to fall into negativity much more easily when trying to impress. Finally, slow or outspoken partners might throw you off your game as well. In this case, you're letting external circumstances affect you too much. Make a refocusing plan to help you deal with these distractions (see Chapter 16)

Q: I practice a lot, but my game has gotten worse. Why?

A: When it comes to practice, quality is more important than quantity. You might practice a lot, but that same commitment might make your game worse. When you don't improve with all the extra practice, you sometimes start questioning your technique. You might make changes in a technique that has worked well for you in the past, and consequently your game doesn't improve. This starts a negative spiral in which you start changing more and more things in your swing, and you wind up confused and discouraged. Practice less, but with more quality. Go through Chapter 1 again to rediscover what a good shot involves. Then, go to Chapter 14 to find out more about quality practice.

Q: Do I need to have a good swing before I start doing some mental training?

A: Absolutely not. You might benefit more from mental training if you already have a good swing, but it isn't necessary. Mental training can help you learn faster and acquire good habits. It's never too early to start thinking well.

Q: I have uncontrollable first-tee jitters. What can I do to stop that?

A: Most of us have a heightened level of intensity on the first tee. You have two choices: either you label yourself as being nervous, or being excited. The physiological response is the same, but it's the psychological tag you put on it that's important. Instead of worrying about butterflies in your stomach, get them to fly in formation. Establish a good preshot routine and adhere to it (see Chapter 12). Also, see chapters on self-talk (Chapter 5), composure (Chapter 8), and concentration (Chapter 9) to help you relax and concentrate.

Q: I can't lie to myself. How can I tell myself that things will be better when it's not the case?

A: It's not a question of lying to yourself. It's a question of perspectives. You have to learn to think like a winner. If you want to limit yourself, fine. But why not try to stretch your limits? You'll see that if you really keep a positive attitude, you will play better. A negative attitude will surely always keep you in mediocrity. It also reinforces negative self-beliefs and attributions. See Chapter 4 to find out more about self-beliefs.

Q: My playing partners are pretty long-hitters and I feel intimidated by them. Is that normal?

A: Long shots may be spectacular and may give you some advantage on certain holes, but that's not what makes you score well. Remember that it's the short game and putting that count most. Go ahead and see how many shots you make within a hundred yards or less on your next round. We each have our strengths and weaknesses. A 230-yard drive that is accurate and consistent is a much more versatile weapon that an erratic 300-yard drive.

Q: I'm already slowing everybody down. I don't want to have a preshot routine that slows people even more.

A: It's a mistake to think that a preshot routine will make you become a slow player. A routine may be systematic and consistent, yet won't slow anybody down if it's a good one. Tell yourself that you will slow everyone down a lot more if you rush your swing and hit another bad shot. What creates slow play are people that are not ready when it's their turn to hit, people that give themselves or others swing lessons before each shot, and people who can't decide on what kind of shot to make or club to choose.

Q: I seem to play better when I don't think about anything. I just walk up the ball and whack it. How can this be?

A: If this is the case, then you're already doing things the right way. A swing that is already well-learned is better left alone. When you try to control an automatic skill, you run into trouble. Keep trusting your swing, and let your unconscious mind do the rest.

Q: My friend doesn't need any preparation and he always plays well. Why is that?

A: You need to remember that preparation is personal. What your friend needs to be well-prepared is different from what you need. Find out what preparation works best for you, then do it before every round (see Chapter 15).

Q: I don't like to be conservative and hit a 3-wood or an iron off the tee. I play better when I'm aggressive.

A: There's a difference between being aggressive and being smart. If you want to hit your driver all the time, then by all means do it. But be ready to assume the consequences. If you're attempting a high-risk shot, then don't get angry if the results are bad. However, if your goal is to score well, perhaps you should play more smartly. Be aggressive when the circumstances are right. If the reward for a risky shot is no better than a less risky one, then choose the more conservative shot. Always weight the risks and benefits of each decision.

Scorecard

Par 72

Front nine score:
Back nine score:
Total score:

The 19th Hole

Congratulations! You've just completed what can perhaps be your most important 18 holes. You've learned how to identify your strengths and weaknesses as well as understood what enables you to execute a good shot and play a good round. You've learned how to set goals to direct your efforts and push you to accomplish things you didn't think you could achieve. You also know how self-beliefs can affect everything you do on and off the golf course. You've learned how to improve your confidence, composure, and concentration through tools such as imagery, self-talk, and relaxation. Then, you've incorporated all those strategies into performance routines and mental plans. Now, you're ready to improve.

The last sentence is extremely important, because there is a big gap between knowing and doing. As such, this book has only given you the information and the tools to improve. Whether you do or not, is up to you and you alone. Like everything else, you need to work hard on it. Mental training is not a magic pill. It takes time and commitment, but at the end of the journey, what a reward it is!

To get the most out of your new mental skills, you'll need to practice and refine them, and don't be worried if some things don't work right away. Refine your strategies and adjust them to suit your personality and playing style. And remember, don't be afraid of trying new things. There is no right or wrong when it's personal. If it works for you, then it's right.

Through this book, you've planted the seeds of excellence in your game. Now, it's time to cultivate your garden of excellence each and every day. If you love the game as much as I do, then I have no doubt you'll accomplish what you only dreamt about before your started reading this book. Hopefully, you'll be able to transfer what you've learned here to your everyday life to truly make this a journey of excellence.

But enough said for now. Get out there and play the best golf of your life!

Appendix A
Charts and Logs

Performance Profile Chart

Quality	Ideal Rating	Current Rating	Difference

Competition Evaluation

A. Think about your all-time best performance and answer the following questions:

1. Circle your feeling *going into this round.*

   No determination   0 1 2 3 4 5 6 7 8 9 10   Completely determined

   No anxiety   0 1 2 3 4 5 6 7 8 9 10   Very anxious

   No physical   0 1 2 3 4 5 6 7 8 9 10   Highly activated
   activation (flat)   and pumped up

2. Rate your level of Confidence in this round:

   No confidence   0 1 2 3 4 5 6 7 8 9 10   Completely confident

   What was the main reason(s) responsible for this confidence level?

3. Rate your level of Concentration in this round:

   No concentration   0 1 2 3 4 5 6 7 8 9 10   Completely concentrated

   What was the main reason(s) responsible for this concentration level?

4. Rate your level of Composure in this round:

   No composure   0 1 2 3 4 5 6 7 8 9 10   Very composed

   What was the main reason(s) responsible for this composure level?

5. What were you saying to yourself or thinking shortly before the start of that round?

6. What were you paying attention to or focusing on during that round?

B. Think of your all-time worst performance and answer the following questions:

7. Circle your feeling *going into this round/hole*.

| No determination | 0 1 2 3 4 5 6 7 8 9 10 | Completely determined |

No determination   0   1   2   3   4   5   6   7   8   9   10   Completely determined

No anxiety   0   1   2   3   4   5   6   7   8   9   10   Very anxious

No physical   0   1   2   3   4   5   6   7   8   9   10   Highly activated
activation (flat)   and pumped up

8. Rate your level of Confidence in this round/hole:

No confidence   0   1   2   3   4   5   6   7   8   9   10   Completely confident

What was the main reason(s) responsible for this confidence level?

9. Rate your level of Concentration in this round/hole:

No concentration   0   1   2   3   4   5   6   7   8   9   10   Completely concentrated

What was the main reason(s) responsible for this concentration level?

10. Rate your level of Composure in this round/hole:

No composure   0   1   2   3   4   5   6   7   8   9   10   Very composed

What was the main reason(s) responsible for this composure level?

11. What were you saying to yourself or thinking shortly before the start of that round/hole?

12. What were you paying attention to of focusing on during that round/hole?

C. What was the main difference between your best and worst performance?

13. In what you were thinking prior to that round/hole?

14. In what you were focused on during that round/hole?

15. How would you prefer to feel before each round/hole?

No determination	0 1 2 3 4 5 6 7 8 9 10	Completely determined
No anxiety	0 1 2 3 4 5 6 7 8 9 10	Very anxious
No physical activation (flat)	0 1 2 3 4 5 6 7 8 9 10	Highly activated and pumped up

16. How would you prefer to focus your attention during each round/hole?

17. How would you prefer to approach each round/hole?

Goal-Setting Form

Skill area to be improved	Specific Goal(s)	Strategy	Evaluation Date	Conclusion

Self-Belief Chart

Negative or Limiting Self-Belief	Replacement Empowering Self-Belief	Behaviors Supporting New Belief

Self-Talk Log

Self-talk Statements	When	Why	Consequences

Self-Talk Change Chart

Negative Self-Talk Statements	Positive Self-Talk Statements

LIST OF PERSONAL AFFIRMATIONS

Personal Achievement List

LIST OF PERSONAL ACHIEVEMENTS

Distraction Control Chart

Critical Moment	Potential Distraction(s)	What to do

Refocusing Chart

Refocusing Cue	Critical Moment

Post-Round Evaluation

Name: Date:

Personal Stats

Total Score:	Front:	Back:
Fairways:	Greens:	# Putts:
Eagles:	Birdies:	Pars:
Bogeys:	Double Bogeys:	Other:

These questions are designed to help you reflect upon your game and to help you develop or refine your routines and game plans.

1. Did you have a performance outcome goal for this event?

2. If so, to what degree did you achieve this performance outcome goal?

Did not achieve goal at all	0 1 2 3 4 5 6 7 8 9 10	Achieved goal completely

3. What was your on-site goal(s) for this round (e.g., what focus did you want to carry into this round?

4. To what degree did you achieve this on-site focus goal(s)

Did not achieve goal at all	0 1 2 3 4 5 6 7 8 9 10	Achieved goal completely

5. Circle your feeling *going into this round*.

No determination	0 1 2 3 4 5 6 7 8 9 10	Completely determined
No anxiety	0 1 2 3 4 5 6 7 8 9 10	Very anxious
No physical activation (flat)	0 1 2 3 4 5 6 7 8 9 10	Highly activated and pumped up

6. Rate your level of Confidence in this round:

No confidence	0 1 2 3 4 5 6 7 8 9 10	Completely confident

What was the main reason(s) responsible for this confidence level?

7. Rate your level of Concentration in this round:

No concentration   0   1   2   3   4   5   6   7   8   9   10   Completely concentrated

What was the main reason(s) responsible for this concentration level?

8. Rate your level of Composure in this round:

No composure   0   1   2   3   4   5   6   7   8   9   10   Very composed

What was the main reason(s) responsible for this composure level?

10. How did your preparation go?

Terrible/ no preparation   0   1   2   3   4   5   6   7   8   9   10   Really well

Were you feeling the way you wanted to feel?

11. What were your thoughts as you approached this round?

12. How did your game plan go?

Poorly/ no game plan   0   1   2   3   4   5   6   7   8   9   10   Really well

What elements of the plan went well, what did not, what needs work or adjustment?

13. What were you focused on when at your best during this round?

14. What were your thoughts before each successful shot?

15. What were your thoughts before each bad shot?

16. Were you distracted at any time during the round?

If yes, what was the cause(s) for this distraction?

17. Did you have to refocus at any time during this round?

If yes, what did you specifically do to refocus?

Did the refocusing strategy work immediately?

18. Review this evaluation form. What lessons can be drawn from this round?

Preparation Chart

Physical Activity	Psychological Activity	Strategy

Pre-Competition Plan

Timeline	Physical Preparation	Psychological Preparation

Critical Situation Chart

Critical Situation	What to do

Appendix B
Relaxation Script

Here is a progressive relaxation script that you can tape and listen to, or have someone read it to you.

Progressive Relaxation Script

Sit or lie down in a comfortable position and try to relax. Close your eyes and take a long, slow, deep breath through your nose, inhaling as much air as you can. Then exhale slowly and completely, feeling the tension leave your body as you exhale. Take another deep breath and let the day's tensions and problems drain out of you with the exhalation [pause]. Relax as much as possible and listen to what I say. Remember not to strain to relax. Just let it happen.

As we progress through each muscle group, you will first tense for approximately 5 to 7 seconds and then relax 20 to 30 seconds. Do not start tensing until I say "now". Continue to tense until I say "OK".

Begin by tensing the muscles in the dominant hand and lower arm by making a tight fist NOW. Feel the tension in the hand, over your knuckles, and up the lower arm..... OK. Simply let go of the tension and notice the difference between tension and relaxation [pause 20 to 30 seconds].... Make another fist NOW [pause 5 to 7 seconds]. OK. Relax. Just let the relaxation happen; don't put any effort [pause 20 to 30 seconds].

Next, tense the muscles of the dominant biceps by pushing your elbow down against the floor or the back of the chair. Tense NOW. Feel the tension in the biceps without involving the muscles in the lower arm and hand.... OK, relax and let it go. Just let it happen.... Tense the biceps NOW..... OK, release it. Notice the difference between tension and relaxation.

With your non-dominant hand, make a fist as tight as possible NOW. Feel the tension in your hand and lower arm..... OK, slowly release your hand, draining all the tension out.... NOW tense again.... OK, relax and feel the difference between tension and relaxation.... Also notice the different feeling for each new muscle group.... NOW push the elbow down to tighten the non-dominant biceps.... OK, relax.... NOW tense again..... OK, notice the decrease in tension and enjoy the feelings of relaxation. Notice the sensations you have in both arms and hands. Perhaps there is a feeling of warmth and heaviness in these muscles. Enjoy the feeling of relaxation.

Turn your attention to the muscles in your face. We will relax the face by progressing through these muscle groups. Begin by lifting the eyebrows just as tight as you can NOW. Feel the tension in your forehead and scalp [pause for only 3 to 5 seconds with these smaller muscle groups]. OK, relax., enjoying the spreading sensation of relaxation.... NOW frown again... OK, release all the tension... Your forehead feels as smooth as glass...

Next, squint your eyes very tightly and at the same time wrinkle up your nose. Tense NOW. Can you feel the tension in the upper part of the cheeks and through the eyes? OK, relax.... NOW tense again..... OK, release all the tension....

Next, pull the corners of your mouth back and clinch your teeth, but not so hard that your teeth hurt. Tense NOW. You should feel tension all through the lower part of your face and jaw. OK, relax...

Next, tense and relax the muscles of the neck by trying to pull your chin downward toward your chest but at the same time preventing the chin from touching. That is, counter the contraction of the muscles in the front part of the neck with the contraction of the back part of the neck. NOW tense. You may feel a bit of shaking or trembling in the neck muscles as you tense them. OK, relax. Drain all the tension from the muscles in the neck.... See if you can get your neck and face to feel completely relaxed. NOW tense the neck again. Feel the discomfort.... OK, relax. Drain all the tension out... Remember relaxation is only the absence of tension.

Take a deep breath and hold it while raising your shoulders upward toward your ears. Tense NOW. Feel significant tension in the chest, the shoulders, and the upper back.... OK, relax. Drain all the tension out.... Hold your breath and raise your shoulders again NOW. This may be a familiar sensation as most athletes raise their shoulders and/or hold their breath when they are uptight. OK, drain all the tension out. Let your shoulders drop completely. Enjoy the spreading sensation of relaxation.

Next tighten your abdomen as though you expect a punch while simultaneously squeezing the buttocks together. Tense NOW. You should feel a good deal of tightness and tension in the stomach and buttocks.... OK, release the tension, gradually letting it all drain out. Just let it happen... NOW tense again..... OK, relax. Feel the sensation of relaxation spreading into those muscles....

Turn your attention to your right leg. Tighten the muscles in your right thigh by simultaneously contracting all the muscles in your thigh. Tense NOW. Try to localize the tension only to your thigh.... Note the sensation. OK, relax. Contrast the tension and relaxation sensations. Remember relaxation is merely the absence of tension; it takes no effort except merely releasing the tension..... NOW tighten the right thigh again.... OK, release the tension. Just let it passively drain out. Enjoy the feeling of relaxation.

Next flex your ankle as though you are trying to touch your toes to your shin. Tense NOW. You should be feeling tension all through your calf, ankle, and foot. Contrast this tension with the tension of the thigh.... OK, relax. Simply release the tension; let go of any remaining tension.... NOW tense again.... OK, slowly release all the tension...

Tense the muscles in your right foot by either pointing the toes or curling your toes tightly inside your shoes, but don't tense too hard or you might get a cramp. Tense NOW. Particularly note the sensation of tension in the arch and ball of your foot. OK, relax. As all the tension leaves your foot, feel the spreading sensation of relaxation... and perhaps warmth and heaviness, or even tingling. All of these sensation are normal. NOW tense again... OK, slowly release all the tension. Let your foot, ankle, and calf feel very relaxed...

We will go through the same sequence with the left leg [provide appropriate commentary during tensing and relaxing phases]. Begin by tensing all the muscles in your left thigh NOW.... OK, relax... Now tense again....OK, release the tension...

NOW flex your left ankle as though you are trying to touch your toes to your shin...OK, release the tension.... NOW flex again... OK, relax....

NOW point or curl your toes... OK, release the tension..... NOW tense again... OK, relax.... Both your left and right leg are now totally relaxed. If you feel tension anywhere in your leg, simply release it.

Relax all the muscles in your body, let them all go limp. You should be breathing slowly and deeply. Let all the last traces of tension drain out of your body. Scan your body for any areas of tension. Wherever you feel tension, do an additional tense and relax. You may notice a sensation of warmth and heaviness throughout your body, as though you are sinking deeper and deeper into the chair or floor. Or you may feel as though you are as light as air, as though you are floating on a cloud. Whatever feelings you have, go with them.... Enjoy the sensation of relaxation....

Before opening your eyes, take a deep breath and feel the energy and alertness flowing back into your body. Stretch your arms and legs if you wish. Open your eyes when you are ready.